Hegel

Hegel

The Restlessness of the Negative

Jean-Luc Nancy

Translated by Jason Smith and Steven Miller

University of Minnesota Press
Minneapolis
London

Selections from *Phenomenology of Spirit,* by G. W. F. Hegel, translated by
A. V. Miller (Oxford: Oxford University Press, 1977), are reprinted by
permission of Oxford University Press; copyright 1977 Oxford University
Press. Selections from *Philosophy of Mind,* by G. W. F. Hegel, translated by
William Wallace, with *Zusätze* translated by A. V. Miller (Oxford: Oxford
University Press, 1971), are reprinted by permission of Oxford University
Press; copyright 1971 Oxford University Press. Selections from *Hegel: Faith
and Knowledge. An English Translation of G. W. F. Hegel's "Glauben und
Wissen,"* edited by H. S. Harris and Walter Cerf (Albany: State University of
New York Press, 1988), are reprinted by permission of the State University
of New York Press; copyright 1988 State University of New York, all rights
reserved. Selections from *The Philosophical Propaedeutic,* by G. W. F. Hegel,
translated by A. V. Miller, edited by Michael George and Andrew Vincent,
are reprinted by permission of Blackwell Publishers.

The University of Minnesota Press gratefully acknowledges financial
assistance provided by the French Ministry of Culture for the translation
of this book.

Originally published in France as *Hegel: L'inquiétude du négatif.* Copyright
Hachette Littératures, 1997.

Published by the University of Minnesota Press
111 Third Avenue South, Suite 290
Minneapolis, MN 55401-2520
http://www.upress.umn.edu

Library of Congress Cataloging-in-Publication Data
Nancy, Jean-Luc.
    [Hegel. English]
    Hegel : the restlessness of the negative / Jean-Luc Nancy ;
translated by Jason Smith and Steven Miller.
        p.   cm.
    Includes bibliographical references and index.
    ISBN 0-8166-3220-0 (alk. paper) — ISBN 0-8166-3221-9 (pbk. : alk.
paper)
    1. Hegel, Georg Wilhelm Friedrich, 1770–1831.   I. Title.
B2948 .N3213 2002
193—dc21   2001006419

Printed in the United States of America on acid-free paper

The University of Minnesota is an equal-opportunity educator and employer.

12 11 10 09 08 07 06 05 04 03   10 9 8 7 6 5 4 3 2

Contents

Abbreviations

Citations of works by Hegel are given with the following abbreviations. When indicated, the translations have been modified in compliance with Nancy's use of the French translations.

LA   *Hegel's Aesthetics: Lectures on Fine Art.* 2 vols. Translated by T. M. Knox. London: Oxford University Press, 1975.

LL   *Hegel's Logic: Part I of the Encyclopedia of Philosophical Sciences (1830).* Translated by William Wallace. London: Oxford University Press, 1975.

PM   *Hegel's Philosophy of Mind: Part III of the Encyclopedia of Philosophical Sciences (1830).* Translated by William Wallace. London: Oxford University Press, 1971.

PN   *Hegel's Philosophy of Nature: Part II of the Encyclopedia of Philosophical Sciences (1830).* Translated by A. V. Miller. London: Oxford University Press, 1970.

PP   *The Philosophical Propaedeutic.* Translated by A.V. Miller. Edited by Michael George and Andrew Vincent. London: Basil Blackwell, 1986.

PR   *Elements of the Philosophy of Right.* Translated by H. B. Nisset. Cambridge: Cambridge University Press, 1991.

PS   *Hegel's Phenomenology of Spirit.* Translated by A. V.
        Miller. London: Oxford University Press, 1977.

SL   *Hegel's Science of Logic.* Translated by A. V. Miller. New
        York: Humanities Press, 1989.

INTRODUCTION

Nancy's Hegel, the State, and Us

Jason Smith

> [O]ne begins by asking oneself if all common existence is
> political or not, if the in-and-as-common should not precisely
> be distinct from the political, which is at most only one aspect
> of it (the one concerning justice and power).... The in-and-
> as-common, which is certainly coextensive with collective and
> individual existence, is not uniquely "political"—or rather, it
> is no longer political in the sense that Plato-Hegel intended....
> There is a disparity of spheres of existence, and this disparity is
> not an empirical crumbling: it must be thought for itself, as
> another type of "unity" than the unity of subsumption under
> the essence of the "political."
> —Jean-Luc Nancy, "Rien que le monde"[1]

> Between Us: First Philosophy.
> —Jean-Luc Nancy, *Being Singular Plural*[2]

What if it became necessary to conceive of common existence in
terms no longer on loan from the canons and catechisms of political philosophy, and therefore with no regard for the latter's
investments in the categories of the state-form, the decisions and
reach of sovereignty, or of the form of law and the juridical sphere
in general? Upon what reserve might one call the moment the
classical styles and modes of thinking the political announce their
status as terminal? In short, what would happen if our being-
together was no longer posed in terms of its inscription within
the system of institutions that structure the totality of what Hegel

called an "objective spirit" (whose essence is found in the internal constitution of the state and in the punctual decision for war), but in the minimal opening of a space whose folds were not yet invested with recognizable contours? What if this recomposition of a new space of the political manifested itself precisely in a kind of proto-political sociality that would *not yet* be political in any identifiable sense, an *ontology* of being-in-and-as-common whose claims could not simply be articulated in inherited political idioms? Finally: what if this swerve away from the institutional structurations of what Hegel called *Sittlichkeit* were to take place in a text titled *Hegel: The Restlessness of the Negative?*

It seems necessary to confront the present text on Hegel with the accumulated gestures that mark all of Nancy's work since the mid-1980s, and more specifically since the publication of *The Inoperative Community.*[3] Whatever the specific results of these analyses and interventions on the theory and essence of the "political," what is most insistent in Nancy's work is precisely its desire to describe a form of originary sociality that cannot be characterized in terms of sovereignty and the law, but as the merest "opening of a space."[4] Such an opening, voided as it is of any essential relationship to the forms associated either with a public sphere or with an agora, does not seem immediately political: in truth, it seems rather bare. It is precisely this barrenness—what will also be described as a nudity, a laying bare, a place of exposure and exposition, a desert(ed) or abandoned space—that Nancy seeks. This nudity is the mark of essentiality: its isolation appears to offer a purified image of the political. But it is precisely this summoning of a pure politics that perhaps forces Nancy to admit that, the moment one attains an absolute politics, the instant one enters into the essence of the political, one lands in a realm that is, strictly speaking, no longer or not yet political. Perhaps all of Nancy's work on the "common" is structured by this paradox: the purely political is nonpolitical.[5] And this is what it means to insist on this strange difference between politics and the "with" of collective existence.

The immediate historical implications of this gesture are obvious, and double. First, we are returned to a certain archaic, matrical structure of being-in-common: the purification is operated through a desedimentation of the encrusted determinations that the political has received across its long history. But this return to a certain origin also touches on what is most urgent in our contemporary, global political space. This is why Nancy's theorization of the political is not simply the representation of an ontological substructure of political forms; it attempts to announce precisely what is happening today to the political. The ferocious deterritorizations of capital, the installation of mediatic networks of an unheard-of density, and the promotion of international law and its reference to "humanity" all conspire in the effective (and not simply theoretical or methodological) dismantling of our system of standard political referents. This eclipse of the state-form and all of its classical determinations—the person of the sovereign, the adherence of this figure to a border and a territory, the concept of citizenship and mythical references to a "people"— is well under way, and it is precisely this shedding of obsolete forms that Nancy characterizes as a laying bare, a denuding, or an emptying. This historical decomposition of the political exposes its essential structure: it assumes the form of an exposed surface, an empty place. It might just be that this spacing-become-global comes after the dissolution of sovereignty in order to occupy, and yet not fill, the empty place of sovereignty: "Th[e] spacing of the world *is itself the empty place* of sovereignty.... The problem concerns the empty place as such, and is not about waiting for some return or substitution."[6] In the *Experience of Freedom,* Nancy hit upon another phrase to describe such a place resisting all appropriation: a space *left* free, abandoned or deserted, left and therefore not taken over. The essential structure of the political therefore presents itself only at the moment of its disappearance: at the moment when sovereignty gives way to what it conceals, namely, a proto-political hollow that is a pure and simple exposure of us to each other. This exposure, in its rarity, has absolutely no content, no signification, and can be evaluated according to no prescribed scheme (good or evil, progress or regression, disappointment or hope). If the desert everywhere grows, and if this must be everywhere denounced, it is still necessary to think what this figure conceals: a deserted space that is the condition of all being-with.

If we bracket, for the moment, the particularly contemporary relevance of Nancy's approach to what he calls the "place" of community, it is easy to note a host of philosophical precedents for the separation of an ontology of being-in-and-as-common and the political. An unlikely one, however, given Nancy's almost total lack of reference to his work, would be found in Husserl.[7] Although the latter would be loath to speak here of an "ontology" (for reasons both axiomatic and too difficult to address here), it is nevertheless the case that his consideration of a field of transcendental intersubjectivity in isolation from all determined and "worldly" forms of sociopolitical existence can be said to shadow Nancy's gesture. This transcendental intersubjectivity, whose constitution is most famously and amply described in the notoriously difficult Fifth Cartesian Meditation,[8] is that stratum of transcendental experience that not only founds every reference to politics and its institutions, but is a necessary portal for any understanding of what it means to say "with" in general. For Husserl, this meant that it was necessary to ask: under what conditions is one permitted to speak, with rigor and responsibly, of alterity in general? Putting aside the fact that even the extended thing represents, for Husserl, an alterity that is already irreducible because indefinite, his conclusion was that it is only possible to speak of the "other" at all to the extent that otherness assumed the form of egological subjectivity, of an other transcendental ego, an other absolute origin of the world: alter ego. This formulation of the problem was, however, only a provisional or indexical one, because the last manuscripts reveal that Husserl increasingly saw the initially autonomous problems of the constitution of the alter ego and that of temporality converging: that the constitution of the other ego

has a temporal form, and is therefore inseparable from the constitution, in the living present, in my present, of another now.
This constitutive relation takes the form of an anticipation or
protention, and this other now dons the guise of an other present "in" (immanent to) my present. This other present is, however, also the other's present. This is why, though Husserl never
states it in exactly this form, one can conclude that the other is
the future in general.[9] This is precisely what Emmanuel Levinas
does (and what makes him Levinas and not Husserl) when he
says, on the first page of *Time and the Other:* "the aim of these
lectures is to show that time is not the achievement of an isolated
and lone subject, but that it *is* the very relationship of the subject
with the other."[10] This *is* records that what is spoken of here is
not, as always the case with Husserl, a simple "analogy" between
temporal transcendence and the "distance of the Other's alterity"
(p. 33), but an identity.[11] But whereas this relation will subsequently
be characterized by Levinas as a preontological, prepolitical, and
therefore ethical relation to the other in general, Husserl would
disqualify this relation as either political *or* ethical. It would be
the mere carrying out of a rigorous description of the relation to
the other in general, within the frame of the transcendental question: what does it mean to say "other," what does it mean for the
other to appear as other at all, and therefore before, strictly speaking, any consideration of a determined relation to that other: a
relation of respect, for example, or violence, of justice or exploitation. "First philosophy" as neither ethics nor ontology.

When Jean-Luc Nancy speaks in his turn of the "place" of community or of being-with as "opening," the apparent poverty of
these descriptions' content marks this opening as pure: an absolute
opening to the other, an absolute opening of being to itself as
common.

In *Hegel: The Restlessness of the Negative,* this place, spacing, or
opening goes by any number of names: the table of contents provides just some. Perhaps the ultimate name is, however, the barely
presentable figure indicated in the text's final chapter: us as

between us. That everything would come down to a preposition, and not simply the exposition of the philosophical content of Hegel's work, points to where the question of style in philosophical writing remains critical.

But is it really so novel to shift the terrain of political analysis away from the problems of the state and sovereignty? Both the Marxist and the Foucauldian traditions agree that the real interest lies elsewhere. Whatever their disagreements on the exact nature of the word's content, they both agree that the problem of the political should be displaced from the formality of juridical structures toward *apparatuses of power.* Their univocal antijuridicism binds them in this common avowal: the juridical form as such is reducible to a means or technique, an instrument or technology. It is possible therefore to conceive of the political in purely instrumental terms: the juridical form becomes a method of exploitation. It is for this reason that the Marxist "tradition" can speak of a "state apparatus," and Foucault of a "political technology."[12] In the case of Foucault, the characterization of the political in terms of technicity no longer allows us to place it in the hands of a determined class; with Marx, however, the "phantasmagoric" form of the law itself is inseparable from its manipulation by that class that has usurped the means of production. Nothing is more fundamental, for Marx, than the necessity to differentiate cleanly between the formal equality of juridical structures and the real inequality of the relations between capital and labor. The conflict that structures the social space of the capitalist mode of production is precisely the contradiction between the *legal* equality of juridical persons before the law and the effective expropriation operated in the extortion of surplus value and the concentration of capital.[13] It therefore stands to reason that when, in a polemical text such as the *Manifesto of the Communist Party,* the modern state as juridical form is characterized as being "power organized in one class for the oppression of another,"[14] it is the state-form *altogether* that is indicted.

It is no doubt the case that, when speaking of the critique of the state-form, and more generally of the "juridical" as the site of the political, reference to a Marxist "tradition" is necessary: it is well known that the volume from *Capital* dealing with the state remains missing. To the extent that there is no theory of the state properly speaking to be found in Marx, it was precisely the construction of a theory of political constitution that preoccupied his inheritors—Lenin's *The State and Revolution* is only the best-known trace of these debates.[15] Whatever the specific inflections given to this problem throughout the tradition, one trait insistently repeats: the disqualification of the juridical sphere as the place of political. From the moment that the legal sphere's simply formal equality is characterized as the repression of a class content, the state can no longer be thought of as the mediation of class interests, but only as the suppression of one in the name of another. It is therefore a simple technique—means to an end, detour furthering a calculable interest—that shelters its own instrumentality under the sign of a claimed universality. Louis Althusser, in the course of his famous essay on what he specifically calls "ideological state apparatuses," formalizes this tradition as follows: "The State is a 'machine' of repression, which enables the ruling classes . . . to ensure their domination over the working class, thus enabling the former to subject the latter to the process of surplus-value extortion."[16] To the extent that the form of law as such is reduced to a technology—and therefore a tool—it paradoxically becomes disqualified as the site of political intervention. Whatever the immediate tactical benefits of parliamentary opportunism, the tradition stemming from Marx has often made the question of the political—that is, of class struggle—inseparable from a critique of every reformist venture cloistered in the juridical sphere.[17]

What has been so disquieting about Nancy's work is therefore the fact that he chooses to think the political in still another fashion, in terms other than those borrowed from the canonical "antinomy" or correlation of the juridical (in particular, the state-form) and power (be it characterized either as the extortion of surplus value or the proliferation of disciplinary techniques). For Nancy, these two options appear to form a specular pair that is neutralized by a third term, what he has variously called "community" or the "ontology" of the common. This neutralization opens onto an absolute sociality: a pure being-with not yet encumbered by any properly political or even ethical determination. It is precisely this characterization of the common as *not yet* "properly" political that has ensured these texts' relative illegibility. Even if Nancy has insisted on the fact that this pure opening is simply the *condition* of the political without itself being political, and therefore that its theorization in no way substitutes for either the analysis of political institutions or the denunciation of exploitation, it is the implied syntax of this formulation—politics without politics—that has proved most disturbing. Bound up with Nancy's critique of any discourse reducing the political to simple techniques or *technologies of power* (and hence the juridical as a repressive machine brandished by a determined social force) is the necessity to underline that the "political," insofar as it is the "place where community as such is brought into play,"

> is *not*, in any case, *just* the *locus of power relations*. . . . I do not wish to neglect the sphere of power relations. . . . On the contrary, I seek only to insist on the importance and gravity of the relations of force and the class and/or party struggles of the world. . . . But there would be no power relations, nor would there be such a specific unleashing of power (there would merely be a mechanics of force), if the political were not the *place of* community.[18]

Nancy insists here on the determination of the political as the "place" of community, while emphasizing that this place must in turn be thought of as irreducible to—*"not . . . just"*—the "locus" of the relations of exploitation, extortion, expropriation, and concentrations of capital and power that no doubt structure almost the entirety of "our" relation to and with each other. This insistence on the problematics of space, place, and local as well as their resistance or irreducibility to a field of implicated forces can be said to constitute the most minimal element of Nancy's developments on the common. It is for this reason that the same concerns reappear later in *The Experience of Freedom:* "[T]he political does not primarily consist in the composition and dynamic of powers . . . , but in the opening of a space."[19] The invocation of a space and its opening communicates with the possibility of an as yet unqualified excess with regard to power. But the mere indetermination of an opening is hardly situated on the terrain of what would be considered the political *properly* speaking.

To characterize this opening as so meager should not, however, suggest that it remains as yet untouched by the ravages of what Marx associated with the political: like Marx, Nancy describes this exposure as the trial of expropriation. But to the extent that an initial "exposition" to the other is constitutive of being-with, expropriation is the pure and simple possibility of any relation to the other *whatsoever*. On this side of violence and peace, nudity and exposition depict the primary structure of sociality in the form of an offering.[20] If there is a certain "expropriation" at the heart of commonality, it is not essentially political in any canonical sense. It may *also* or eventually take the form of an exacting of surplus value, but its *exemplary* instance is totally other. Social existence facilitates

> access to what is *proper* to existence, and therefore, of course, to the proper of *one's own* existence, only through an "expropriation" whose *exemplary reality* is that of "my" face always exposed to others, always turned toward an other and faced by him or her, never facing myself. This is the archi-original impossibility of Narcissus that opens *straight away* onto the *possibility* of the political.[21]

Nancy no doubt develops a very nuanced, stratified structure: if this *impossibility* opens straight away onto the *possibility* of community, the apparent directness or immediacy does not at once communicate with the political proper, only touching on the latter's "possibility." In all classical rigor, a condition of possibility is topologically defined by its nonparticipation in the field it opens. As such, it stands to reason that this pure and simple possibility is not yet political. If being-common is not "immediately" political, it is the fragility or the plasticity of this "not" that commands every delimitation of the space of the political *strictu sensu*. But it is the "sense" of the political that is here at stake, as well as its striction: that is, the limits within which it is restricted and restrained, the locales or places to which it is confined or delivered.[22]

If formerly Nancy had to insist on the manner in which a thought of "community" in no way replaces more classical styles of political discourse and intervention (even if it must necessarily impact that redefinition of their very "objects"), today he is inclined to emphasize the necessity to dissociate them in a way that nevertheless remains enigmatic: "if one likes, the ontology of the common is not immediately political."[23] "Not immediately" is made to communicate with the "not just" and the "not yet" of a simple condition of possibility of the political, but the negativity of these "nots" still requires clarification. What seems incumbent is a questioning of the precise style of this separation, keeping in mind the manner in which the delicacy of this partition always threatens its recoding according to classical schemes that Nancy has spent the entirety of the last two decades forestalling.

In the meantime, it is already possible to see a smile breaking out on Hegel's face. The negativity of this "not . . ." (immediately, yet, just, etc.) that separates ontology from politics already has a name: mediation. In a pulverizing embrace, Hegel and Nancy are in accord.

In a sense, when Nancy speaks of a space of community that is "not just"—and therefore "not yet"—political in the reduced sense of the agonistic play of violent interests, he is not only adhering to the most classical determination of the political in the Western tradition, he is also virtually subscribing, in its barest elements, to the Hegelian concept of the political over and against the Marxist critique. Virtually, because he never says as much explicitly, nor does he, as already mentioned, develop his analysis of community or "being-in-and-as-common" using the

conceptual armature Hegel deduces from this minimal definition: state, sovereign, war. In this way, then, Nancy remains
crypto-Hegelian, but only to the extent that what is appropriated
from Hegel is only this purest form of the political imaginable:
the staggeringly barren possibility that the "true end" of political
unity is nothing other than "union as such."

The reduction of the form-of-law to a means and instrument—a political technology—has as its target the classical interpretation of political constitution as an "end in itself." This
tradition is congenital with the West, and marks its initial for-
malization in the Aristotelian exhibition of the political in terms
of the "supreme finality" (or "nonuseful finality") of living well
(eu zein).[24] It is no doubt with Hegel's *Philosophy of Right* that
this inheritance is accomplished: for the absolutely minimal ma-
trix of his theory of political sovereignty rooted in state power is
his contention that the "security and protection of property and
personal freedom" cannot be the final destination of the political. The state comes to name, for Hegel, precisely the thought of
the political in which the unity of collective existence would not
have as its end the simple regulation of the (violent) play of particular interests at its heart. To the contrary, the political in the
guise of the state comes to be its *own* end: what is proper to the
political is that it have no extrinsic orientation, no end falling
outside itself. The answer to the question, What is the "end" of
political unity? can therefore only be met with this tautological
response: "*union* as such." When Hegel formulates the difference
between state and civil society in precisely these terms, one
imagines a kind of proleptic and symmetrical rejoinder to
Marx's own critique of the philosophy of right:

> If the state is confused with civil society and its determination is
> equated with the *security and protection of property and personal
> freedom* [my emphasis], *the interest of individuals [der Einzelnen]*
> as such becomes the ultimate end for which they are united; it
> also follows from this that membership of the state is an optional
> matter.—But the relationship of the state to the individual

> *[Individuum]* is of quite a different kind.... *Union* as such is itself
> the true content and end, and the vocation *[Bestimmung]* of
> individuals *[Individuen]* is to lead a universal life. (*PR* §258,
> Addition)[25]

Hegel's concern in this text is to characterize the state not as a means or instrument to "protect" the rights and freedoms of individuals or determined social groups; to the contrary, the state is a "substantial unity" that is an "unmoved end in itself" (§258). As a result, it is only in the transindividual institution of the state that freedom "enters into its highest right": the state as that space of social articulation in which freedom is most free. As a result, the state has priority over the individual, and therefore its right supersedes the individual's own determined rights and freedoms. It is therefore inevitable that these "rights" would come into conflict, and that the assertion of the right of the state would suppress the rights of its members. But, for Hegel, this opposition is only apparent. For it is precisely at the moment when the individual submits to the law that it is most free; it is precisely at the moment in which its own rights and freedoms are given up that the individual manifests its true freedom—this moment is called war.[26] In taking leave of the simple being-for-itself of its unilateral determination, the individual demonstrates its freedom in losing it; its supreme freedom is therefore indistinguishable from its "*highest duty*... to be [a] member of the state" (§258). The contradiction between the "highest right" of the state and the determined rights of individuals is therefore an identity. If initially it appears that their freedoms are negated in their submission to an institution, this neglects the fact that such an individual freedom is one-sided, subjective, and therefore merely freedom in itself, not yet effective and real, and therefore not yet free. To the extent that the state is defined as "objective spirit" over against the interiority of the individual, the making real of freedom is also the negation *of* freedom. It is only in the humbling, lowering submission of the individual that the latter is paradoxically *elevated* to the status of one possessing true, because effective, freedom.

This passage from the *Philosophy of Right* does not, however, appear in Nancy's text. Or not patently. For there is a moment, at the beginning of the final chapter of the book ("We"), where Nancy explicitly cites the description, lexicon, and argument of this passage while dropping all reference to the state. This elision is, moreover, consistent with the entire gesture of the book. It is as if dropping the name and figure of the state would be the first condition of any renewed engagement with a Hegelian thought of the political that is today too often the butt of bad jokes. This strategy of appropriation is completely justified from the perspective of Nancy's own, "signed" corpus; but what happens when, in writing a text "on" Hegel whose terminal chapter is titled "We," one refuses all reference to the theory of the state, or any explicit reference to the entire problematic of *Sittlichkeit* and its triadically implicated moments of family, bourgeois society, and the state? This is the perhaps the most riddling dimension of *Hegel: The Restlessness of the Negative:* it succeeds in *suppressing virtually all references to the state.*

The passage on the difference between civil society and the state does, therefore, appear once in the text, on the condition that no reference to the state is made. It occurs at the very opening of the final chapter ("We"), and its language is immediately recognizable. Nancy is in the course of dispersing the consensus that reads the negation of individual rights and freedoms as a sheer loss of freedom rather than its effective realization:[27]

> Hegel has often been read as if he exhibited the auto-development of an anonymous Subject or a Reason, foreign to us, the big Other of an autistic Self that, moreover, would only be the fantasmatic correlate of the subject of *a proprietary and securitary individualism*—two subjects each the mirror for the other, each as stupid and wretched as the other. (76; my emphasis)

This is the only moment in *Hegel* where the passage on the state and civil society appears, under a modified form. It is clear that the reference to and critique of a "proprietary and securitary individualism" demonstrates that Nancy has this passage in mind at this moment. The journalistic image of the state or the political as a "big Other" is not so much a strategy to disqualify Hegel as an attempt to ensure that the sense of the political never be at stake: that the only option for thought or practice be the civil liberties of a liberalism unashamed of its ties to the totalizations of capital. Hence, what Nancy here renders a specular "correlation" is classically deemed an opposition—the Hegelian figure of the state as "big Other" can only be countered and completed by the liberal fetishizations of individual rights and freedoms. But if Nancy's intention is to protect Hegel from this charge, he seems able to do so only at the expense of dropping all reference to the state at the very moment he appears to cite the language of a passage in which Hegel defines the state over against the conception of governmental and legal institutions as the simple management of determined interests and "subjective freedoms" (*PR*, §258, Addition).

The basic strategy behind Nancy's dropping the reference to the state seems to follow a double logic. It can be argued that Nancy's developments on the "political" in his own, "signed" corpus follow a logic that is "crypto-Hegelian," at least to the extent that it refuses to reduce the political to an "apparatus," and therefore refuses to confuse the space of the political with the mechanics or dynamics of power relations. If sides were being chosen, he would be, in this very specific sense, on Hegel's side. But, once again, from the moment he assumes the lexicon and descriptive traits of Hegel's text while offering no explicit reference to the passage he is secretly citing—and this in a text *on* Hegel—it is obvious that some equivocation is announced. Not retaining the name "state" is, however, not innocent: the political institutions of objective spirit, and par excellence the state, can in no way be conceived of as secondary elaborations of a fundamental stratum of being-in-and-as-common. There is, quite simply, no separation of ontology and politics in Hegel: the common is not simply elaborated in the state, it is realized. Thus, from the moment Nancy assumes the minimal definition of the "political" in its most abstract, least developed form—nothing more than "union as such" as its own end—without developing its implied moments (especially those of internal and external constitution, sovereignty, and war), it is hard to mark where Nancy speaks of Hegel otherwise than as a simple inheritor of the tradition of the political stemming from Aristotle. In short, from the moment the name "state" is removed, the name Hegel itself seems eclipsed.

The only other relevant reference to the state in the entire book is less stealthy, but still marginal. In the longest footnote of the book, Nancy gives some justification for his treatment of Hegel's political philosophy. It is precisely at this point that a stratification within the structure of the political is announced. The "we" of the final chapter will not be identified with the state, but with what Nancy calls either the "common" or "being-with-the-other." It should be noted in advance that these terms, and this division, mark an intervention in the reading of Hegel:

> Love is [in §535 of *PM*] said to be the "essential principle of the State." This does not define an amorous politics, and it supposes that Hegel thinks "the State" as the *sublation* (or upheaval) *[relève]* of the apparatus of separated power that we designate with this name. In other words, he exposes what will become into our time the primary political theme: no longer the institution and nature of government, but the contradiction of the separation and non-separation of the "common" considered for itself— and also, consequently, the contradiction of separation and non-separation *within* being-with-the-other itself. Consequently, through his incontestably naive and dated confidence in a certain model of the State, Hegel also provides the lineaments of a thought of the contradiction of every philosophical *foundation* of the political. But we cannot dwell on this point here. (p. 119 n. 11)

If one brackets the initial reference to "love,"[28] the interpretative moves here seem fairly legible. Once again, it is a question of releasing the Hegelian determination of "the state" from what *we* confuse with it: that is, from the simple governance of competing private interests, from the simple safeguarding of determined rights and freedoms. But because the Marxist theory of the state as "apparatus" reveals the regulatory vocation of the state to be a concealed suppression of one set of interests in place of another, it is necessary to underline that what "we *designate* with this name" is precisely the *negation* of what Hegel "thinks" with or "through" this name. As a result, when reading Hegel, it is necessary to perform a double gesture. On the one hand, it is necessary to recall that our use of the term *state* and Hegel's are completely different: we call "the state" the very thing Hegel says it should not be "confused" with. The avoidance of this confusion is the first justification for the dropping of the name "state": the only way we can think what Hegel meant by or through the term *state* is to shed the term and its sedimentations. This is not all; for Nancy later insists that the term was already a compromise within Hegel's text, and that its appearance there is almost an accident: a simple capitulation to epochal and contextual pressures. In attempting to think this essence of the political, Hegel can only approach it through the by now historically obsolete trope of the state; but in expressing it through such a figure, he ensures the definitive retraction of this "essence" (or "essential principle") beneath its epochal format.[29] Hence, we must initially recall that the "state" in Hegel does not mean the "apparatus" of power we associate with this term. But in a second movement, it is for this very reason necessary to drop the term altogether in order to encounter a proto-political configuration that is only hinted at in the initial distinction between the state ("union as such") and civil society. What Hegel is the first to think is the "'common' considered for itself," that is, precisely, an "ontology" of being-in-common that is to be thought "as such," beyond or in the place of "the state" and of sovereignty. But he thinks—and this is the problem—the "as such" of the common only insofar as it appears *as* the state.

If this thought of the common "for itself" or as such requires the subtraction of the term and figure of the state, this operation is not simply assignable to Nancy. It is what history has done to Hegel's text: a novel layer of legibility opens up at the precise moment when the dominance of a certain model of the state is pronounced over. History itself—if we know what this means—has dropped the name "the state" from Hegel's text, thereby revealing what was to be thought through it and in its stead. From now on, the word *state* means that clearing whose opening it formerly occupied. It will be necessary to think the common for itself.

When Nancy speaks, in the Preface to *The Inoperative Community,* of *subtraction,* he appears to have a certain aporia in mind. In saying that "community is made or is formed by the retreat or by the *subtraction* of something," he indicates that this something is community itself.[30] To the extent that community is "made" through or as "subtraction" of itself, the operation or event becomes indistinguishable from an experience of mourning: "community is revealed in the death of others; hence it always revealed to others."[31] The structure of its phenomenality shades into its disappearance: the community reveals itself at the very *instant* of the others' death, that is, at the instant when there is no longer any community. Such is the irreducible constraint structuring the communitarian exigency, that community not be a substance hiding beneath its appearing, while its appearing can only be its occlusion: it is there, effectively present, only in the movement of its withdrawal, recession, retreat.[32]

If Nancy's work on community has not been articulated around the problems of the law, sovereignty, or the juridical sphere in general, nor has it opposed to these themes an analysis of the "techniques" of power, it is because these have been replaced by love and by mourning (in *IO*), or even, at the limit, by the "archi-original" exposition of a face.[33] This set of terms is not "political" in any classical sense, but forms a constellation whereby a pure sociality that is the condition of the political can be made to appear. The differentiation between the ontology of the common and the political *strictu sensu* raises a number of questions, and first of all, the precise nature of this difference. The most immediate problem our text poses is, however, the extent to which such a separation can be located in Hegel himself—in short, where an ontology of the "we" can be developed in such a way that no essential reference is made to the problematic of objective spirit, at least in the latter's encyclopedic formatting. Would we be privy to a simple operation performed from without on the communal flesh, one removing the extrinsic debris that was called the juridical, political, and "forms"—forms that are simple screens cloaking what Christopher Fynsk calls the "grounds of the social or political bond," grounds that would be identified in Nancy's latest texts with either an analytic of *Mitsein* or a transcendental intersubjectivity in the Husserlian style?[34]

Hegel's own response, not only to Nancy's own project but to the reading proposed in *Hegel* as well, would probably be to assimilate these types of "foundational" (though this word is extremely inadequate) discourses to the formalism with which Kant was reproached. He would no doubt recall that the classical articulation of these two strata assumes the form of a hierarchization that in turn implies a purification and separation. From the moment one separates the ontology of being-in-common from the political, one effectively performs an evaluation: separation and difference always means order. Ontology has always meant a discourse treating the "really real";[35] it cannot avoid introducing a criterion discerning contingency from what is essential. The latter becomes the theme of "first philosophy," while the former can be reduced to empirico-anthropological debris whose sedimentations are always potentially removable to the extent they remain simple constructions. To take Husserl alone: the fields of *Sittlichkeit,* of the family and the political and the sciences of spirit (history and the analysis of social structures), might give rise to eidetic disciplines with their specific style of rigor and scientificity, but their worldiness prevents them from being anything other than "regional" concerns. This very regionality subordinates them to an analysis of the structures of the transcendental ego in whose enlarged immanence they are constituted in their noematic irreality. The transcendental ego is not worldly, because it articulates the entire field of constitutive regions and types into a nondeductive system. Even when, in his most profound departure from a Kantian transcendental idealism, Husserl develops a transcendental theory of the constitution of the alter ego (with all the attendant aporias), the purity of this structure is as yet unaffected by the institutional fields of kinship, belonging to a people, co-citizenship: in short, the relation to the other is in no way reducible to its inscription within a family, a genealogy, the transmission of names and legacies, the inclusion in a world determined otherwise than in its perceptual infrastructure. Hegel would therefore probably respond that what binds Nancy's own discourse to those of Husserl and Heidegger, and therefore to Kant, is its "formalism."[36] And, consequently, its more or less hidden complicity with empiricism. Not only does this imply the reduction of these cultural and spiritual formations to historical accidents or dross with no internal principle of organization or rationality; this very expulsion mutilates the philosophical exercise itself insofar as it deprives it of the possibility of thinking the rationality and necessity of these institutions at all. The net effect of such a separation of the ontologico-transcendental from the political, the denial of the intrinsic rationality of these institutions, Hegel would argue, not only reduces philosophy itself to a regional discourse retaining no hold on or sway over the political as such, it also deprives philosophy of its very end or destination— its effective existence. Hegel would agree, no doubt, that ontology is not *immediately* political: philosophy is always political philosophy, but the joint of the copula by no means implies simple homogeneity. Their identification refers not, once again, to a transhistorical, formal, and analytic inclusion, but to the effective labor of a concrete synthesis that cannot be said to take place in history, but whose becoming is, properly speaking, nothing other than history itself. This synthesis, in being historical, is nevertheless a priori: it could never be reduced as such, or subtracted.

Let us imagine Nancy's response. It would perhaps consist in the refusal to assimilate the "subtraction" of the political from the common to a mere truncation: a refusal of the identification of this subtraction with the evacuation of a determination or content in view of unveiling a simple *form* that would be, like all form, a pure construction or, at best, a "moment" that, being the negation *of* all content, would call for the very content whose negation it is. In short, if there is a certain negativity in this subtraction, it refers not to a form, but to *an opening* or *a space*. This space, if it is to be left free,[37] cannot be the "nothing" of a content, and therefore the determinate negation of some content to come. If the topological structure implied by every ontologico-transcendental condition implies a negativity—the condition of the political is nothing political—the true enigma is nothing less than the negativity of this "nothing." Not being a determinate negation of a "political" content, it is not an abstract negation either. The encounter with the other takes place only in the stripping bare of every cultural predicate: love is indissociable from the *nudity* of the other's taking place. This encounter must take place in secret: because love is, here, only the experience of mourning, the other comes only to disappear. But beyond the nudity of this encounter, there is the barrenness of a space. The description of this space would coincide with the latter's essential desertion. Being essentially exposed and exposure, it is only a pure opening that closes the moment it receives any determination or content— in the instant and movement itself of its gape. This abandoned or deserted space—and Nancy elsewhere refers us to this essential desert, this essential desertion[38]—is marked by its poverty; but such a poverty is confounded with the generosity of its expanse. Irreducible to all form and to all content, this space must be *left* free to the precise extent that it resists all appropriation, every taking. Its poverty signals no privation; its want provokes, in the last instance, no desire. Having nothing to offer, it only gives itself; it is only the absolute resistance to all appropriation and therefore to all violence or power. This space is not yet the other; it is the merest opening toward which the other will or will not come. We encounter each other in secret: Nancy says, in the final chapter on the "We," that this encounter takes place as our "just-between-us *[entre-nous]*" (p. 79). We come between us.

If such a space must be left free, what would Hegel have left to teach us? Inversely, what, in the insistence on or of such a space, would be left of Hegel?

Hegel

The Restlessness of the Negative

Restlessness

Hegel is the inaugural thinker of the contemporary world. His entire work is penetrated and mobilized by the consciousness and
by the feeling of having to make a decisive inflection in the course
of the world, and consequently, in the course of philosophy. Sense
no longer offers itself in the religious bond of a community, and
knowledge is no longer organized into a meaningful totality. But
community gives way to society—which, from now on, knows
itself as separated from itself—and knowledge is the knowledge
of objects and procedures, none of which is an end in itself. This
world perceives itself as the gray world of interests, oppositions,
particularities, and instrumentalities. It therefore perceives itself
as a world of separation and of pain, a world whose history is of
one atrocity after another, and whose consciousness is the consciousness of a constitutive unhappiness. It is, in every respect,
the world of exteriority from which life withdraws, giving way to
an endless displacement from one term to the next that can neither be sustained nor gathered in an identity of meaning. Never
again can this displacement regain the movement of a transcendence that would raise it toward a supreme signification. It knows
the possibility of a "death which has no inner signification,"[1] that
is, the possibility of the death of signification itself. The transcen-
dent—being raised high beyond its pure and simple given—has
distanced itself in the void of abstraction. Those who claim, re-
actively, to restore its dignity lose it that much more surely in

sentimentality, or in the fanaticism of pretensions to posit the Absolute here and now.

An absolute negativity of the Absolute appears to constitute all experience of this world and its consciousness of itself. But it is the world's experience and its consciousness: this experience and this self-consciousness could no more be withdrawn from the world than one could "overleap [one's] time."[2] This is no morbid complacency, no preference for the virtues of unhappiness. But this world needs truth, not consolation. It must find itself in its ordeal and by way of its restlessness, not in the solace of edifying discourses that do nothing but pile on more testimony to its misery. But "finding itself" can in no way consist in presupposing a soul, a value, and an identity that would have simply, and provisionally, been overshadowed. "Self" cannot precede itself, because "self" is precisely the form and movement of a relation to self, of a going to self and a coming into self. This world not only has a consciousness of separation: it is in separation that it has consciousness of itself and the experience of this consciousness.

Still more exactly: it is because the world undergoes itself as a world of separation that its experience takes the form of the "self." This form is that of a relation and a movement. "Self" means "relating itself to itself": it is a relation whose terms are not given. And the world of separation is that world in which the terms of a relation of sense—terms such as "nature," "gods," or "community"—are no longer given.

Hegel takes it upon himself to think how the obscure knowing wherein this world undergoes itself is knowing of the *self* as non-given relation, or infinite relation: how, consequently, what (or the one whom) he names *subject* is revealed in this relation, and how the subject constitutes and liberates itself in the dimension and according to the logic of the negation of the "given" in general.

The Hegelian *subject* is not to be confused with subjectivity as a separate and one-sided agency for synthesizing representations, nor with subjectivity as the exclusive interiority of a personality. Each one of these can be *moments* among others of the *subject*, but the subject itself is nothing of the sort. In a word: the Hegelian subject is in no way the *self all to itself*. It is, to the contrary, and it is essentially, what (or the one who) dissolves all substance— every instance already given, supposed first or last, founding or final, capable of coming to rest in itself and taking undivided enjoyment in its mastery and property. The reader of Hegel who does not understand this understands nothing: he has surreptitiously presupposed an ideological notion of the "subject"—a notion that is nonphilosophical, individualist, egoist, and "liberal"— or, a notion no less ideological, "communitarian," nationalist, or imperialist.

The *subject* is what it *does*, it is its act, and its doing is the experience of the consciousness of the negativity of substance, as the concrete experience and consciousness of the modern history of the world—that is, also, of the passage of the world through its own negativity: the loss of references and of the ordering of a "world" in general *(cosmos, mundus)*, but also, and thereby, its becoming-world in a new sense. It becomes immanent, and it becomes infinite. This world is only this world; it has no other sense, and it is in this way that it is the world of the history-of-the-world (history is sense as movement of negativity, but it does not itself have a sense that would bring it to an end). At the same time—and it is this that is *time*, the concrete existence of negativity—this world, the realm of the finite, shelters and reveals in itself the infinite work of negativity, that is, the restlessness of sense (or of the "concept," as Hegel names it: restlessness of conceiving-itself, grasping-itself, and relating-itself-to-self— in German, *begreifen:* "to grasp," "to catch hold of," "to comprehend"). It is in this way, in the restlessness of immanence, that the spirit of the world becomes. It neither seeks itself (as if it were for itself an exterior end) nor finds itself (as if it were a thing here or there), but it effectuates itself: it is the living restlessness of its own concrete effectivity.

Spirit is not an inert being, but on the contrary, absolutely restless [*unruhig*: "troubled," "agitated," "restless"] being, pure activity, the negating or ideality of every fixed category of the abstractive intellect; not abstractly simple but, in its simplicity, at the same time a distinguishing of itself from itself; not an essence that is already finished and complete before its manifestation, hiding itself behind its appearances, but an essence which is truly actual only through the determinate forms of its necessary self-manifestation.[3]

This world of movement, of transformation, of displacement, and of restlessness, this world that is in principle and structurally outside itself, this world where nature does not subsist but steps out of itself into work and into history, this world where the divine does not subsist but exhausts itself beyond all its figures—this world moves toward no end or result other than itself, nor toward a resorption or sublimation of its own exteriority. This does not mean, however, that it is the brute fact of simple erratic positions of existence: in that case, the restlessness of self-consciousness would not itself be a dimension of its experience—or, more exactly, there would be neither experience nor thought. Restlessness is itself already thought at work, or at stake.

This world is therefore not a simple result, nor does it have a result. It is the world that itself results *in* its own movement, and the thought of this its own truth is itself, in turn, a movement and a restlessness—the very same, in fact, to the extent that it is restlessness of self, for itself, and uneasy about itself; and because it reveals itself as other, infinitely in the other. Hegel's thought thus becomes philosophy transforming itself, and, in Hegel's wake, the acts and discourse of philosophy have never ceased explicitly turning themselves outside of themselves, and/or returning into themselves to their ungroundable ground, never ceased rehearsing or re-creating themselves as much as denouncing and exasperating themselves.

Ordeal, misery, restlessness, and task of thought: Hegel is the witness of the world's entry into a history in which it is no longer just a matter of changing form, of replacing one vision and one order by some other vision and some other order, but in which the one and only point—of view and of order—is that of transformation itself. It is thus not a point; it is the passage, the negativity in which the cutting edge of sense gets experienced as never before.

Since Hegel, we have not ceased to penetrate into this negativity; and the time of Hegel himself, along with his philosophy, have in their turn been left far behind us. In a certain sense, we can no longer cull from them any readily available signification. Which is why, moreover, we do not here claim to "restore" Hegel, nor do we expound a "Hegelianism": we read Hegel or we think him such as he has already been reread or rethought up to us, such as he has already been played out in thought. But what Hegel first gives to think is this: sense never being given nor readily available, it is a matter of making oneself available for it, and this availability is called freedom.

Becoming

Hegelian thought does not begin with the assurance of a principle. It is simply identical to the restless, preoccupied, and non-presupposed return into itself of philosophy that exposes itself to what it already is: the movement of the consciousness of this world that knows itself as world, and that no representation (image, idea, concept, or determined sense) can saturate or reassure, because, to the contrary, the world bears them all away into its history.

The restlessness of thought first means that everything has already begun: that there will therefore be no foundation, that the course of the world will not be stopped in order to be recommenced. It means that one is no longer in Descartes's element, nor in Kant's, and that, if the thread of history is broken, this happens of itself, because its very continuity is only division and distension. But all is equally already finished, finite: the infinite or the absolute will be presented in no determined figure. There will be other figures, but they will now be known for what they are: successive forms in passage, forms of passage itself, and forms born away by passage. The finite figure thus presents, each time, only itself—itself and its infinite restlessness.

In these two ways—absence of beginning and absence of end, absence of foundation and absence of completion—Hegel is the opposite of a "totalitarian" thinker. But he does think this: that the truth is total or it is nothing (and this is what the word "system" means for Hegel: it is the holding together of the whole of truth), and that totality is not a global form, assignable as such and liable to be foisted upon being as well as sense, but the infinite self-relation of what is.

Hegel, therefore, does not begin with a principle or with a foundation. Such a beginning would still remain foreign to the movement and passage of truth. For philosophy, he writes, "the beginning has relation only to the subject who decides to philosophize."[1] But the condition of the decision is the subject itself insofar as it is undetermined, or insofar as it is "abstract will, infinite for itself in its immediate singularity."[2] Thought is a decision—practical, like every decision—of the infinite subject that decides for this infinity itself, that is to say, that decides not to hold to any finite form of being or of itself. Philosophy is not essentially a theoretical knowledge or interpretative proposition: it is the praxis of sense.

Every beginning that would not be in decision would be a given beginning, and thus already derived, produced elsewhere—like the simple abstract notion of "being" or like the idea itself of a "principle." But every beginning in decision is not a beginning: it is an upsurge in the course of the given, a rupture, nothing that could be posited as such. And each subject has to break off in its turn: each one is just such a rupture.

Hegel neither begins nor ends; he is the first philosopher for whom there is, explicitly, neither beginning nor end,[3] but only the full and complete actuality of the infinite that traverses, works, and transforms the finite. Which means: negativity, hollow, gap, the difference of being that relates to itself through this very difference, and which *is* thus, in all its essence and all its energy, the infinite act of relating itself to itself, and thus the power of the negative. It is this power of the negative that inhabits the gap where relation opens, and that hollows out the passage from presence to presence: the infinite negativity of the present.

It has often been said: Hegel gave himself everything in advance, he presupposed everything, he presupposed the Whole that his

System then pretends to discover. Hegel is playing with us; he makes the whole thing into a comedy—the comedy of the tragedy of separation.

But this argument turns against itself. Hegel, if one likes, presupposes the absolute. But this presupposition is made precisely in order to ruin all presupposition or pre-givenness. To be in the absolute is, purely and simply, to be; it is being there, *hic et nunc*. The Hegelian "presupposed" is the real, absolutely—and with it, in it, the reality of sense, that is to say of the subject in which and *as* which the real comes to posit itself as such, comes to be known by a knowing that is not only the knowledge of an object, but the knowing and grasping of self. In me and as me, the universe knows itself or grasps itself as universal, just as, in each thing, I know myself and grasp myself as singular, and vice versa. This has nothing to do with some mystical effusion: it is the simple reality of manifestation in general. And this, as a matter of fact, is the absolute presupposition, which is to say that this precedes every particularity, every determination—though not as a generality, a principle, or an origin, but as the very concreteness of being. In the same way, the knowing and grasping of self precedes every posing of a question, every discursive articulation or thesis.

This thought does not question. It does not ask why there is something, nor how our knowledge is possible. To the precise extent that it does not proceed from a question, it does not proceed from the presupposition concealed in every question. This thought consists in exposing and explicitating what is real in it (Hegel says it outright: *Auslegung des Absoluten*)[4] but only insofar as exposition and explicitation make themselves part of the real and are the movement of being in itself and for itself. Exposition, explicitation, or interpretation is the "self-exposition of the absolute and ... [the] display of what is."[5] It is a matter of letting the absolute expose itself. Nonetheless, this thought is not a passivity: self-exposition is the very nature of the absolute. Letting the absolute freely expose itself is nothing other than putting thought into play—and to work—as freedom. This intimate connection of thought and being—since Parmenides, the oldest concern of philosophy, and its sole program—this absolute conjunction of freedom and necessity bears all the weight of the Hegelian enterprise, and all of its gravity and difficulty. In the final analysis, this enterprise can be a matter of nothing other than dissolving these categories of "thought" and "being," or of making and letting them dissolve themselves. But this dissolution is itself nothing other than the operation of each one toward the other. Each deposes the other of its own consistency and subsistence. But it is in positing the other that it deposes it—and that it deposes itself in this deposition. The operation of sense thus gives itself as pure negativity—but this negativity is nothing other than the upsurge of the real in its absolute concreteness, nothing other than the point of the subject.

No respite, no repose outside the inscription of this point; there you have Hegel's restlessness—but still: this point is nothing other than restlessness itself . . . it is, at the same time, the unsettling, and the unsettled.

Knowing, then, will not be a representation (*Vorstellung*: positing of an object before and for a subject of knowledge, conforming to its "vision of things," that is, to its meager limitation), but a presentation (*Darstellung*: "position there," put in place and on stage, exposition, upsurge of the being-subject as such), and consequently the negation of every and all given presence, be it that of an "object" or of a "subject." Not given presence, but the gift of presence—such are the stakes.

Something is there, given (for example, this book).[6] As given, this thing is only a thing other than all the other things: negation of the others, negated by them. I know this thing as there and as given (I know it at the same time as real and as only a possible in the real). In this knowing, the thing is no longer there, but is exposed, posited as known (for example, again, in this book). The first negation is negated. But my knowing is itself a being-given-there that cannot remain given without being exposed in its turn (it is necessary to take leave of the book...). The one and the other, thing and knowing, must be exposed and mutually expose themselves to one another—exposing, at the same time, the necessity and the simple possibility of their reality, or its contingency. There is no determined thing that, through its determination, would not be in this necessity of its contingency, which is to say, in the "absolute restlessness of becoming."[7]

Now, there is no thing—neither being nor thought—that is not determined. Everything is in the absolute restlessness of becoming. But becoming is not a process that leads to another thing, because it is the condition of every thing. Its absolute restlessness is itself the determination of the absolute. Becoming is quite exactly absolution: the detachment of each thing from its determination, as well as the detachment from the Whole in its determination. And it is thus that the absolute is what it is: equal to self and, consequently, in absolute repose—but it is so only thus, quite exactly, as nonrepose. And the process or progress of the absolute is an infinite process or progress.

An infinite process does not go on "to infinity," as if to the always postponed term of a progression (Hegel calls this "bad infinity"): it is the instability of every finite determination, the bearing away of presence and of the given in the movement of presentation and the gift. Such is the first and fundamental signification of absolute negativity: the negative is the prefix of the *in*-finite, as the affirmation that all finitude (and every being *is* finite) is, in itself, in excess of its determinacy. It is in infinite relation.

This is first of all what thought reveals, and what it neither questions, founds, nor represents. But that thought neither questions, founds, nor represents—this signifies that it does not work from the outside of things, but is itself the restlessness of things.

To be sure, it is not immediately this restlessness, nor is this unrest a simple property of things: Hegel provides us with neither an animist magic nor a pantheist fog (to the contrary, he leads the most dogged and energetic of struggles against all the forms of pantheism that burdened his age). If thought was not separated from things, it would not be thought, nor would there be restlessness. Thought, to the contrary, is the separation of things and the ordeal of this separation. But thought is thus itself the separation of things from thought—judgments, concepts, significations. It runs through their separation, and it separates itself from their separation—as relation itself and, better, as the restlessness of relation, as its restless love.

Penetration

Philosophical decision thus clearly signifies that it decides neither for faith nor for knowledge, but that its decision consists precisely in separating itself from both. What Hegel calls "knowing" or "science," and "absolute knowing," opens modernity as the age of the world that can no longer posit the relation to sense or truth as either immediate or mediate. It is not that sense or truth is simply lost, has collapsed, or been perverted in the bad infinity of relativisms. Hegel resolutely turns his back on every kind of nostalgia, that is, on every kind of comfort drawn from the image of a given but past sense, given as past, and past as given. But, inversely, this is not in order to place his trust in a new given that would have to be given or give itself in the future, or even as the future itself. Neither past nor future present, but naked present: that is, stripped down to the point of its coming, in the instability of becoming.

This point of the present is neither to be "believed in" nor "known." It is to be experienced, if this is how one wishes to put it, but this experience is neither a simple sensation nor a sentiment. It is the passage of thought through the point itself. The point is the passage. It is not only the passage from a "one" to an "other," but the one, in this passage, finds its truth in the other, and thus touches upon [toucher à] and unsettles its own ground: "the significance of [the Concept's] becoming, as of every becoming, is that it is the reflection of the transient into its *depth* [*Grund*] and that the first apparent other into which the *other* has passed constitutes its *truth*."[1] Now, such a passage is exemplarily that of being into thought: in truth, every passage is the passage to thought or to sense—but reciprocally, every thought is passage to the being of the thing in its truth. One cannot rest content with reducing Hegel to his well-known, too well known, sentences on the truth of the acorn in the oak. For the tree itself is still a passage, and it also has its truth in a fallen and crushed acorn that will never take root, simple disseminated concretion.

This is why thought is penetration into the thing, a breaking or sinking into the thing. The Hegelian *ground* is neither fundament nor foundation, neither groundwork nor substrate. It is the depth in which one is submerged, into which one sinks and goes to the bottom. More precisely, this ground founds only to the extent that it sinks in itself: for foundation should be a hollowing out. Thus thought is not grasped in its depth without being such a hollowing out. Still further: this hollowing neither attains nor brings to light a secure groundwork. It hollows out the point of passage, and the point itself is such a hollowing out: work of the negative, but right at the surface.

Thought thus manifests from out of itself its profound affinity with things. This affinity is brought into play at the most exterior surface of language; *Dinge* (things) and *Denken* (thinking) sound one like the other, one right up against the other: "*Things* and the *thinking* of them—our language too expresses their kinship—are explicitly in full agreement, thinking in its immanent determinations and the true nature of things forming one and the same content."[2]

Nevertheless, thought sinks into things only to the extent that it sinks into itself—which is its own act of thought. Thought that does not think itself is not yet thought, that is, it is not what it must be as thought. On the one hand, indeed, it still lacks an

object: itself. But, on the other hand, this object that it lacks—
the subject—is precisely what makes of thought a thought, that
is to say, not the reformation of a content for work outside itself
(image-thought, sentiment-thought, or notion-thought), but the
penetration of a thing by a sense that would be its own, and that
would be itself.

In order to be such a penetration of sense—of sense into the
thing and of the thing into sense—and in order therefore to be
veritable thought as much as true thought, thought should not
be the instrumental procedure of a formal rule that would lead
the qualities of the thing back to some unity of representation,
according to ready-made categories. There again, the given is in-
valid (the given of concepts, of judgments, and of argumentation).

When I ask what a flower is, I have to presuppose this "being"
according to the given categories of a botany or a horticulture, of
an aesthetics, a symbolism, or even a mysticism. I will thereby only
ever obtain diverse and determined "floralities" that remain exclusive of one another. But now it is a matter of not presupposing and not obtaining anything other than the real of a flower—
that is, indissociably, the "a flower" that I say: "the Idea itself and
suave, absent from all bouquets,"[3] but also such and such flower
here and now, rose, daisy, or pansy [pensée]. To do so, it is not
enough to claim that "the rose grows without why."[4] For this is
still a thought, precisely a thought, and even a thought of the
ground of the thing (as groundless), but a thought that, as such,
has not yet *passed* into the thing, and into its depth.

Thought is able to posit its difference with the thing only to
the extent that it also posits—that it knows, thinks, and exposes—
this difference itself as the passage from the one to the depth of
the other. The poet or the mystic says or shows nothing else. But
philosophy says this saying and shows this showing so as to not
leave them to their immediacy: it is the supplementary turn in
the passage to the depth—the trope that, in its turn, exhausts itself in its own exteriority (in this discourse, here, as in that of the
philosopher in general), but that in exhausting itself shows, on

the edge of its thought, the flower not given but posited in existence—that is to say, steeped in its infinite and concrete truth.

A thought that would not arrive at this concrete unity of the thing would not be a thought. But it can arrive there only in being, at once, the infinite task of thrusting itself into the thing and of denying its separation as mere "thought." The poet's naming is still the index of the "absent." Thought will therefore be—herein lies its being and its concreteness, its act and its praxis—the beyond of the name that the name itself names and in which it annuls itself: the presence of this absence. Presence of this absence as such, effective negativity—effectivity that has blossomed into negativity.

"Thought in *thinking* penetrates the object"[5]—and this is not an abstract or imaginary penetration "in thought." It is not a represented penetration that would remain before what it penetrates, as its finished product. The one who penetrates is himself penetrated, for thought is the thought of being itself, and not "mine." Insofar as it is "mine," my thought is contingent and passes into its other. But to the extent that it has this exterior form of the "I," it is just as much the universal of the for-itself (of the pure relation to self) that penetrates the determinate in-itself, in other words, that makes it enter into the *relation* that is its truth. But it is thus the in-itself that penetrates in itself.

Whatever in this formulation might seem like a homecoming and an Odyssey of the universal spirit should be immediately given the lie by this: on the one hand, the return is made nowhere else than to the depth, to the hollow of existence, and, on the other hand, there is no Ulysses, no single and substantial figure of the subject. But the one who penetrates into himself is each time an other, and its relation.

The form that Hegel privileges is indeed that of the circle, but this circle is a "circle of circles"; not the simple disposition of the same that always comes down to the identical, but much rather, at the same time, both the ground of all circles, the pure movement of the point that turns—"negativity...constitutes the *turning point* of the movement of the concept"[6]—and the ceaseless movement that leaves nothing at rest. Point and movement are indeed the same thing—but only insofar as this "sameness" has no identity other than infinite relation. The equidistance of the points on a circle from the center is the equality of their singular agitations, and the center is their common vertigo.

Logic

The pure element of sense or of truth—what Hegel calls "concept" or "grasp" from the point of view of its activity and the "idea" from the point of view of its presentation—is the element of "spirit," which names infinite relation itself, the step out of self into the other of all reality. This "life of the spirit" is not something separate; it is not a spirituality that floats above and beyond materiality. It is nothing—or simple abstraction—as long as it remains considered in itself as if it were outside the world of effectivity. It is the breath of spirit, but this breath is not an immateriality: on the contrary, it is the unsettling of matter inseparable from matter itself, the sensible insofar as it senses, is sensed, and senses itself. It names the restlessness and awakening of the world, immanence always already tense, extended and distended within itself as well as outside itself; space and time, already, as the ex-position of every position.

Spirit is not something separate—neither from matter nor from nature, neither from the body, from contingency, nor from the event—because it is itself nothing other than separation. It is separation as the opening of relation. This also means that relation does not belatedly happen to pre-given singularities, but that, on the contrary, singularities and relation are one and the same gift.

Every given unity, as simple self-subsisting unity, is only ever a given: something derived, deposited—a moment, unstable like every instant, in the movement that gives relation, in which relation gives itself. The unity of spirit is thus that of this infinite movement, and this unity is never a unicity: it is the unity of the one that never goes without the other and, further, the unity of the one that goes to the other, of the one that *is* only this *going to* the other. The other is itself, in its turn and at the same time, a "one" that goes to the other. At the same time: that is, in the sameness of time that is the difference of the ones from the others.

Thought is not something separate, for "thinking" this "life of spirit" is to actualize relation. Certainly, thought as such represents equality, or rather, it posits equality as such: the correspondence that relation implies. I think this is (equal to) that. And truth should always appear as the resolution of relation into "transparent and simple repose."[1] But this is only one side, the one that corresponds to the detachment of thought insofar as it must hold the truth in front of itself, and in front of us. That is what gives it its air of assurance and impassivity, of complete mastery. Nonetheless, the resolution of relation can be nothing other than the movement, the activity, and the life of relation: not its being, but its going, its coming to pass. To *truly* think that this *is* that, my thought must *pass* from one into the other. "Transparent and simple repose" is thus also "the Bacchanalian revel in which no member is not drunk."[2] The assurance of thought is inseparable from its restlessness—and its restlessness, as drunkenness, is at once an anxiety and an exhaltation, the risk and the transport of relation.

The assurance of thought—its self-certainty—is not imposed on its restlessness like a mask, any more than it comes over it as an appeasement. Nor are the one and the other like the two faces of Janus; and it is imprecise to speak of them as two "sides": what thought is certain of is its restlessness, just as what unsettles it is its certainty.

If thought is indeed the position of equality, posited as the equality of the thing with itself, thought cannot be equality kept in itself, the calm statement that A = A and that I = I, as if this very equality did not immediately, imperiously, and violently call for the exposition of every singularity as such, incomparable and absolutely unequal at the very heart of universal equality. Thought is not therefore equality that keeps itself in itself, but equality that takes leave of itself by virtue of its very equality—of its universality. *Logic* is thus, from its most elementary stage onward, from its first and poorest abstraction, a tearing of identity out of itself, its dislocation, and its alteration—and, this being the case, it is nothing other than the rigorous thought of that by which the identical identifies itself.

There is nothing illogical about this logic; it is not a mad, perverted, or acrobatic logic. With the name "logic," Hegel reclaims what has continuously constituted the *logos* of philosophy—and thus reclaims what has engendered every logic: *logos* signifies that no identity is given, that no unity is simply available, and that identity and unity are always, in their very simplicity and absoluteness, the movement of self-identification and self-unification. *Logos* designates the "making" of every "given"—that is to say, its "giving" and, more precisely, its "giving of itself": thus, *logos* designates the identical not as substance but as act. Its act is that of equality that in equaling itself out makes itself unequal to itself (one must say "in equaling itself out" and not "in order to equal itself out" because equality is not a goal set in advance, but the movement of identity, its identification). If $A = A$, it is because A posits itself as other than itself. And this is precisely what "$I = I$" exposes. *Logos* is subject, which means the exposing of the infinite exposition of identity.

Thought will therefore be equality that takes leave of itself in order to enter into the inequality of the thing. Penetrating the thing, equality will make itself *its* equality, but in thus becoming *its own* it will remain just as much a singular identity, distinct from all the others, as identity identical to every other identity: set in motion and agitated, moved and upset by the same making-itself-identical.

Penetrated into the thing, penetrated by the thing, thought disappears as separate thought. But its disappearance is its conservation, because what it properly is, is separation—and relation. Separation is henceforth the posited presence of the thing: its alterity. What thought posits is alterity in general: point, stone, light, or person as other—which is also to say, each time, this point, this stone, this light, this person. There is nothing indistinct, and thought is the position of absolute distinction. The Hegelian world is the world in which no generality subsists, only infinite singularities.

Neither generality nor particularity subsists, for the "particular" is still only the finite in an extrinsic relation with the general, itself still exterior and therefore in its turn posited as particular—the finite, therefore, in the relation of particular interests with a general interest.[3] The singular, on the contrary, is the finite in itself and for itself infinite, for which there is no separate universality. If I say, "Socrates is a man," I take Socrates for a particular case of the human species. But Socrates-the-singular is not a case: it is he and nothing other. If one prefers, he is an absolute case, and the absolute in general is made up solely of absolute cases and of all their absolute relations.

But singularity does not subsist, or its subsistence is identical to its upsurge, that is, to its punctuality, and therefore to its negativity. What posits the distinct, and identifies it, is separation. Thought penetrates the thing and invades it with separation: its penetration is an emptying. The thing thought is the thing hollowed out, voided of its simple compact adherence in insignificant being. It is only as thought, penetrated by thought, that the flower flowers *as* flower: but this blossoming is the full bloom of negativity made *its own*.

What this thought thinks is the blossoming of the absolute at the heart of the thing. But one should not be misled by this flowery formula. Hegel says, "the rose in the cross of the present,"[4] and the present is self-division: such is its blossoming. Nor is it a matter of substituting absence for presence, of plunging real presence into an abyss—that would in turn be only an ineffable and terrifying hyperpresence. It is a matter of yielding neither to the facile graces of a rosary of sense, nor to the fascination of a stag-gering annihilation. Neither purely present (and thus evanescent) presence, nor purely absent (and thus imposing) absence, but the absolute of presentation.

Thought as thought of the absolute is nothing other than the heir of Kant. With the latter, reason came to know itself as the exigency of the unconditional. Or, more precisely: as unconditional exigency of the unconditional—of which philosophy has be-come the observance and exercise. The refusal to give up on this exigency: this is Kant's thought repeated and taken over by all his successors. Hegel intensifies it to its breaking point, sharpens it to the point of making it breach and tear apart every consistency in which the determination of a conditioned entity retains itself.

The world that knows itself to be immanent is, at the same time, the world that knows itself unconditionally obliged to give sufficient reason for itself. Kant maintains this necessity within the order of an ought-to-be, in which the reason for the world is infinitely separated from itself. But this necessity can still, for Kant, take the form of a wait and can postulate, within this wait, the infinite approach of satisfaction. Hegel, on the other hand, posits that this "duty" itself, the "thought" alone of this duty, of its separation and infinity, has already of itself, in opening time and dividing substance, given rise to the subject.

It is not that there would be no further "duty" to be done and that all is fulfilled, but that the unconditional is no longer merely an end sighted in an infinitely receding distance—it is already in the flashpoint of its absolute exigency. The fact that the absolute is already there and that it knows itself being already there is not an achieved satisfaction, nor some primitive accumulation of sense. This only signifies that the exigency of the true is itself true—even, as is only right, to the extent that this exigency has something excessive and infinite about it: even to the extent that it puts the subject outside itself. The unconditional or the absolute is in no way a supplementary, supererogatory, or even exorbitant dimension that it would be best to leave in the remove ever further removed, ever displaced, of an ideal "kingdom of ends" (or, as one will later say, a "horizon" of values). The absolute is doubtless exorbitant: but it is immediately exorbitant, here and now, opening the present, opening space and time, opening the world and the "I," and throwing existence into its restless exigency.

Not thinking this irruption of the unconditional amounts to not doing justice to *thought:* it is to hold it back from itself—back from the absolute dignity that it posits and from the no less absolute freedom it demands.

The penetration of the thing therefore signifies the penetration of being by this exigency, but not as a well-intentioned impulse that would traverse the order of the given without transforming it, and that would remain suspended in its flight as a sublime elevation foreign to the actual world. The penetration of thought is not traversal, but the concrete hollowing out of concreteness itself. Kant did not give up on its exigency; Hegel does not give up on its effectivity—that is to say, on its effectuation. Not that this effectuation could ever be represented in such and such a given, in this or that "figure" of the absolute. But what cannot be represented does not flee ever farther away into an ideal sky: on the contrary, it is the point hollowing itself out at the heart of effectivity.

In its penetration, thought is not content with opening separation and infinite relation, as if these were "only a thought" and "only an exigency." Thought rather becomes the will to this separation and this relation: the will to determinate concreteness and to the work of its relation to others.

Present

It might seem easy to state, in Kantian terms, that Hegel once again, like the old metaphysics, confuses the Ideas of reason with objects of experience, whereas the careful critical distinction of the two orders is alone capable of respecting the exigency of the unconditional. This would nonetheless be to forget that Kant himself was able—and had—to advance the thesis that the supreme Idea, the Idea of freedom (or reason as such and for itself), arises in experience.[1] Which means that Kant himself could not not do justice, albeit in an uncertain and enigmatic fashion, to what is not simply a desirable consequence of the absolute, but its very condition: its effectivity. Freedom is not something wished for, as Kant knew well, nor is it a formal disposition. It is effective irruption into the effectivity of the world, and the irruption of this effectivity itself. Hegel therefore sets out to think what Kant demands.

It might then seem equally simple to say, in Hegelian terms, that Kant is stuck at "bad infinity," whereas Hegel posits the infinite in and as act, effective here and now. This would, however, suppose that Hegel was content to think and posit this act as a given (as when one claims, with confusing vulgarity, that Hegel assigns an end to history). But the act of the infinite is anything but a given. It is, indeed, rather that by which the given is given. It is its condition, not only of possibility, but of effectivity: its very gift—which is to say, the gift of its manifestation, of its coming to existence. Thought thus sets out toward the given, not simply to submit it to exterior conditions of intelligibility, but in order to penetrate it with what gives it, and what is for itself nothing given: with the negativity of its donation, its upsurge, or its creation.

This is why the Hegelian thought of the absolute in effectivity—because it is utterly contrary to the "totalitarian" delirium that would show here and now the given face, form, and empire of the unconditional—gathers itself up in its entirety and stubbornly immerses itself in the austere discipline of firmly maintaining negativity as the very opening, itself concrete, of the concrete, and as the joining of separation and relation that makes the world the true world.

From this perspective, philosophy does not add a sense or truth that it would have derived from elsewhere than this world itself. It even does nothing, initially at least, other than expose the finite as finite—the infinite finitude of every "form of life." And it is thus that philosophy "paints its gray over the gray" of an aging world.[2] It is not only that Hegel, in his time, experiences such an aging, and the coming of a transformation. It is that thought never has to predict or prefigure novelty—which is or which will always be the novelty of the absolute itself. This would be to reduce novelty in advance to a given, to make of the future a present—and consequently, at that very moment, a past.

But, no more than it preconceives the future, philosophy does not belatedly order the past into a signification. In coming "late," philosophy comes itself as the end that comprehends itself as end, that is, as the penetration of a "form of life" by its own truth: by its passage and its opening toward an other. Not, once again, that the other keeps in reserve the truth of the first, which would be put off until still later. But the truth is at the same time the fulfillment of the form and the testimony that it grants to itself, as well as the grasping of this: that a fulfillment, in exposing itself and in passing, exposes anew the infinite availability of sense, of the gift of sense that thus effectuates itself.

Even while Hegel appears to experience (like his entire epoch) the nostalgia for forms that would have once attained a plenitude of sense now irremediably lost (so went the "beautiful Greek city"), and even while he appears to hail the birth of an accomplished form of the "ethical Idea" and of community (which form the organic State of constitutional monarchy)—and beyond the fact that these two appearances are also for him, without a doubt, two simultaneous tendencies or inclinations that would be incompatible if they had to be upheld together as pure theses—nonetheless, everything shows that the veritable stakes are to be found neither in the pathos of loss nor in that of foundation. These romanticisms—that of the past and that of the future—only skirt, as epochal traits, the rigorous exigency of philosophy: that the present be revealed for what it is, as the restlessness opened between the twilight of a fulfillment and the imminence of an upsurge.

Without a doubt, Hegel deciphers his time as the time of such a present—of such a presentation of the present, of its instability, its tearing, and its passage. The gray of the concept over the gray of the world reveals, with the end of the colored figures in which it was given, the restoration to existence of the task of thinking itself, by itself, beyond all consistency of the figure. But the present—Hegel's as much as our own, and Hegel's that ours perhaps completes—therefore erects no overarching figure. It is not the time of an apotheosis outside of time and of a parousia of the absolute. It is what each time is for itself: the grasping of its passage, which means at the same time self-affirmation *and* the restlessness of the other.

That a time among others posits and thinks itself *as such,* and that it therefore, with Hegel, posits and thinks itself as the time of philosophy, does not make it more exceptional than any other—and above all renders it neither final nor original. This means that this form as well—that of the restless grasping of self and of negativity posited for itself—surges up as a moment. In the word and in the thought of "philosophy," Hegel grasps at once the absolute repetition—the eternal return—of spirit returning to itself *and* the determination of the concept that is still only a concept, of thought that is only gray thought, and still merely "philosophy."[3] But this determination is also what opens itself all the more to the exigency that spirit pass anew into the other, and return to itself from the outside of another determination.

As for the present moment, it is at the same time a moment like any other—passing, like any other, into the other—*and* the moment that grasps itself as moment, naked opening of history that lets itself be glimpsed, for an instant, as simple hollowing out and as act of negativity. It is the moment of the absolute thought as such: as absolution, that is, as unbinding, detachment, and laying bare—not as absolutization. It is the absolution of separation and of relation: everything is at the same time separated and in relation, everything is only separated and in relation. It is this absolution that Hegel named "history," and for which, our time, completing Hegel's, advanced other concepts, that of "technology," for example (and perhaps already beyond this word, the liberation of still another, necessarily unknown, form).

What is asked of thought, consequently, is nothing other than this: to not give up on the inscription of the absolute in the present, such that no present, whatever its form (past, present, or to come), is absolutized. With Hegel, philosophy attempts neither to represent the Whole nor to found it; but it does have the task of opening for itself the totality of relation such as it opens itself in every thing—but as it opens itself, each time, here and now.

Here and now, the totality of relation represents itself as equal—to nothing. The world is simply equal to itself, but in this equality it only confronts its inequality and its exteriority. Previously, the inequality in the world was equal to the inequality between the world and its divine realm. Presently, the world is equal to itself and thus to its own inequality, which exposes itself as the violence of interest and of subjectivity, each of them one-sided.

Everywhere equal to itself, the abstract subject contemplates the exploitation, hunger, distress, and anguish of concrete subjects. Not only is it powerless, but it is the powerlessness of its abstract and empty equality that it opposes, as a paltry infinity, to the misfortune of the world. This name itself, "the subject," has become the name of its own passing out and away, or the name of an empty aspiration and a vain agitation in which "spirit" exhales what might still be left of its last gasp. In place of spirit, but as its final truth, the world knows itself to be the actuality of (and responsible for) extermination, and to be the potential to destroy itself.

Hegel's most famous passage is this:

> But the life of Spirit is not the life that shrinks from death and keeps itself untouched by devastation, but rather the life that endures it and maintains itself in it. It wins its truth only when, in utter dismemberment, it finds itself.[4]

Since Hegel, there have been men who thought that their mission was to endure the death of millions in order to ensure the pure life of spirit—and likewise there is a part of humanity that thinks (in acts, not in discourse) that the impoverishment and exclusion of the rest of humanity is necessary to actualize the only life capable of history and knowledge—or, at any rate, of the concentration of capital.

In a sense, everything happens as if the spirit of the world were executed as Hegel thought—and as if, in fact, there were nothing in the world but the life of its death.

We know with Marx that there is no answer to this death in the consolations of religion—when they are not rather consolidations of the devastation—nor in the abstraction of the legal subject. Marx himself thought nothing other than the effectivity and praxis of Hegelian spirit. But we also know what, in Marx, became confused with the absolutization of a figure.

Consequently, it is possible that Hegel's sentence—the whole of his thought—is as a useless and dangerous pathos. But then nothing remains to be thought other than the powerlessness of all thought. For this sentence not only condenses Hegel's thought; it enunciates what happens to thought in itself and for itself as soon as sense and truth are not presented to it as *given*. If this thought is vain, one is left only with the renunciation of the unconditional and of reason itself; one is left with the various complacent manners of modulating a nihilism.

But it is also possible—there is no other possibility—that it remains necessary to rethink this thought, to sink into it, not as if it were a determined and given thought, but as the very opening of sense and truth, and thus going beyond it by going into it. All true thought, since Hegel, has done this, with him, against him, beyond him.

(This alternative cannot be abstractly decided. No one, not Hegel, nor anyone else, can demonstrate what "true thought" is. It is itself the matter of the decision for "true thought.")

At the very least, one will initially think that the sentence on life in death, insofar as it is a sentence, a proposition, still holds "spirit" at a distance from the "dismemberment" in which it "finds itself." As sentence, it is not yet—or it is already no longer—the thought of what it enunciates. But it enunciates precisely this: if spirit "finds itself" in "death," it is because death is not before it, and not outside of it, neither as the death of an other, nor as the death of self that would remain outside of itself as the simple exterior cessation of the sense of self. Spirit is not a given that looks upon and suffers death as a given other or as another given—and, in this sense, nowhere, not even literally in Hegel himself, is there a spirit of the world that would coldly contemplate the passing procession of deaths and annihilations as the spectacle of its own sense. Spirit is not something finite that would have its own end—its absolute dismemberment—before it as an object, a representation, a duty, an ideal, or an absurd contingency. Without a doubt, it does have this end before it as an object, insofar as it determines itself, and insofar as it can and should say: "death," "the world," "thing," and again, "myself." But, in saying it, and because it says it, spirit posits that it does not have its truth as one thing over against other things.

How spirit is the finite that finds itself to be infinite in the exposition of its finitude, this is what is to be thought—which is to say, this is what it is to "think."

And this is how the truth of sense is the affirmativity of the restlessness of the negative: its insistence in itself, without renunciation or evasion, its praxis, and the *conatus* of its being.

Manifestation

Philosophy is not one more representation, nor one more knowledge. It is not a knowledge of principles or of ends, as if principles and ends were concrete or ideal things over and above other things. Neither is it a reflection upon knowledges, as if these latter (in the widest sense: sciences, technologies, arts, beliefs, sensations, feelings) must be submitted to another knowledge and another evaluation that, in the last instance, would be of the same order as they are, and would demand yet another, higher or more profound, appreciation. Philosophy is neither "high" nor "profound": it holds itself strictly at the height of things, the world, and man. And it does not adopt any "point of view" on them, neither from above nor from below. In a general way, philosophy consists in not adopting any point of view—in not even being a "view" at all, if there is no more "view" once one penetrates the thing, or grasps it.

But the thing at stake is not that thing there, deposited in isolation and enclosed in itself, nor being pure and simple. A thing such as we represent to ourselves a stone to be, or the pure idea of "being," is itself only a derivative given: it has been produced and deposited through an operation. If the stone or being has always been there, it is precisely this *having always been there* that does not go without saying. Or, more exactly: if the thing does go without saying [*va de soi*], the point is that somehow it *goes*—*starting* with itself, *taking leave* of itself, and giving *itself* of itself. Not mere being, but its coming or its life. Hegel names this "the *factum* of physical or spiritual . . . vitality"[1]—and this fact is the "thing itself" that thought penetrates, that philosophy grasps.

This fact is not the fact of one given among others, be it the first one. (*Faktum* is to be distinguished here from other German terms that name the "given" or the "simple fact.") Doubtless, this fact is primordial, but only to the degree that what is primordial, or originary, cannot be anything real, but only the real itself in the making *[le faire du réel même]*—its "making itself of itself." A "making itself of itself" is given from the outset—and it is precisely not a given. One could say: it is a *fiat,* a creation. It would be right to say that Hegel, after Spinoza and Kant, thinks nothing else than what has become of the creation of the world once there is no longer a creator given, nor one to be invented. The *Faktum* is: the thing gives itself. This fact is absolute, insurmountable: one can only ignore it or penetrate into it. It is here that the decision to philosophize comes into play.

That the thing gives itself is a "vitality." It is not organic life, nor just some animation. Vitality is the character of bearing itself outside of itself. The thing gives itself, it bears itself outside of itself, it manifests itself. The "phenomenon" is not appearance: it is the lively transport of self and the leap into manifest existence. Manifesting itself, it is in relation. It singularizes itself. Every thing is singular, and the totality is also singular: it is the singularity of manifestation itself. The singularity of manifestation, or of the world: it is that singularity manifests itself to nothing other than itself, or to nothing. Manifestation surges up out of nothing, into nothing. The manifested is something, and every thing is manifested. But there is no "manifester" that would be yet another thing than manifestation itself. Nor is there a spectator to manifestation. Me with my knowledge, I am also in manifestation: I am manifest and I manifest, in turn, that I am manifest. Manifestation is therefore of itself or it is of nothing; it is of itself as much as it is of nothing.

It is in this sense that truth—which can only be the truth of the *Faktum,* or the *Faktum* itself grasped as truth—is *beyond* every mode of erudite or sensible apprehension of the manifested. It is not beyond as something else, but as the nonthing of the thing, and the nonbeing of being. To penetrate the thing is to penetrate its manifestation, to penetrate the *Faktum;* and, consequently, it is to penetrate the negative as such, or the *nihil* of creation without creator.

Every apprehension is already in itself such a penetration, and the most naive knowing can behave like the most speculative when it believes itself to be in the thing itself, identical to it, unconscious of being over against it.[2] And the same happens when sensing means simply becoming the thing sensed—the scent of a rose or the yellow of a wall.

Sensibility is nothing other than the relation of manifestation to itself; there is no nonsensible manifestation, and thus all truth is in the sensible: but it is there as negativity. Sensible representation indicates of itself that its truth is "in" it as well as "outside" it: this is what "sensing" and "being sensed" mean, and this is what it means that there is sensing, consciousness, representation, and knowledge in the world. Knowing does not come into the world from elsewhere than from the world itself—as the relation of the thing to the negativity of its manifestation, of its "coming from itself."

Sensible representation is being-for-an-other. What it indicates of itself is that this being-for-an-other is the movement of the truth of being in itself and for itself. It indicates relation as negativity of the self, or the self as negativity of relation: true being negates its simple being-self.

To penetrate negativity demands "another language" than the language of representation. The latter is the language of separation: the language of concepts in their fixity, of propositions and their copulas; it is the language of signification. This language is quite simply language itself, and there are no others—or there are only many of them. To speak the other language—that of thought—

is not to speak a mysterious extra language. But it is above all not to enter the ineffable. It is *to think:* to say within language what language does not say; to make language say the identity of subject and object, unless this identity is precisely what it never says, if "to say" is to signify (via the exteriority of signifier and signified). Thought is not language: it is beyond it, beyond the exteriority of the relation between word and thing. But, at the same time, it also is language: it works like a language (such as the English or the German languages), as it articulates things in the play of their differences.[3]

Language says things, it does not say itself—that is, the universal relay of differences whereby language speaks. To say this relay would be to say the passage of determinations into one another, to exhaust every last signification: which is what is proper to thought. The "language" of thought is indeed the exhaustion of determined signification.[4] It is thus identically the exhaustion of the exteriority of language, and the exhaustion of the separate determinations of things: language of penetration into manifestation.

We must hold that the language of thought is a language, or language itself, just as much as we must hold that it is infinite exhaustion and alteration of language. We must hold to this, not only out of the imperturbable and obstinate seriousness of the philosopher who wants to enunciate the unenunciable, but also because only language, exposing itself of itself as infinite relation and separation, also exposes this being-of-itself-outside-itself-in-the-other that is manifestation. In a sense, language is manifestation: it posits the thing outside of itself. It manifests manifestation. But it manifests it as other than itself. Thus, in another sense, language as such names everything and manifests nothing. It indicates in naming, and in the insignificance of names, that manifestation is its truth and its limit.

The language of philosophy is language itself spoken in its infinity; which is also to say, at each instant, at each word, at each signification, language is put outside itself, insignificant or more-

than-significant, interrupted and strained toward its own negativity—toward the "vitality" of "the self." Not language speaking
about itself, but penetrating in itself. Nothing other, in the final
analysis, than what language as such does at each instant, in the
fold of its articulation and in the hollow of its enunciation.

Such is the penetration into sense, which can no longer be
named "sense" in any determined sense: its truth is to be the negative that relates each determination to the others, and only thus
relates it to itself. To penetrate manifestation—or to think *revelation,* as Hegel formulates it, taking from "revealed religion" what
it itself indicates as its truth outside its representation—is to
penetrate into nothing other than the "self" itself, for itself. It is
to penetrate this: that the self is manifest of itself, and it is consequently of itself outside itself. The self is what does not possess
itself and does not retain *itself,* and is, all told, what has its "itself"
in this very same "not" itself: nonsubsistence, nonsubstance, upsurge, subject.

Philosophy is thus the self-knowing of negativity even as it is the
knowing of the negativity of self. No verbal acrobatics here, no
perverse discursive indulgence. The reciprocity and the reversibil-
ity of the self and of the negative form what is to be thought: the
very thing that Augustine posited in the *interior intimo meo,* or
that Descartes did in *ego sum,* but this time undoing, unraveling
all consistency of the *interior* or of the *ego.* The only presupposition of the *self* is that it cannot presuppose itself. Each thought
puts this knowledge at stake: it can only be each time singularly
at stake; it is the concrete singularity of thinking.

The self reveals itself to be nothing other than *negativity for itself.* But negativity for itself is not a thing, considered in its relation to itself or in its return in itself. Negativity is precisely—to
the extent that it "is," or that it can be posited by this word—the
"for-itself," because the "for-itself" is not a relation or an intention that would have a given subsistence in view. "Self" is noth-

ing that preexists "for-itself," and being "for itself" is to be "for" this absolute non-preexistence.

To let this "for" stand on its own as such is to liberate the self—which also means to liberate freedom itself. For this is to unbind the self from every determination to which it would be attached: that of a substance or that of a subject in the sense of a given personal identity, that of an individual or a people, that of some essence or of a symbol, of a signification, of a form, or of a figure. But it is not to unbind the self from all attachment so as to let it float, abstract, in an indetermination that would still only be the void of the "I = I." It is to operate its unbinding and its liberation right at singularity, and for singularity. That I am unbound of myself so as to be precisely this one, such a one exposed to the others and surging up at my empty place: this place that is not caught in the chain of significations, but the place where a subject of sense breaks in, and out of which it surges up.

A subject of sense, this means first off: a sense for each and every one, coming back to the one only insofar as it passes to the other. If "I" surge up, each time, as the identity of the universal and the singular—"I" being nothing other than an upsurge, a throw of sense in itself, without determined content—this takes place only insofar as "I" is shared out equally between everyone. Not only as an equal property of all the speakers-and-thinkers, but as this property that comes to nothing other than to suppress itself as the distinct property of speaking and thinking, as property of a consciousness-over-against, in order to regain itself outside itself, outside of consciousnesses and significations, as manifestation itself, turned back into itself, itself manifested for itself: absolutely liberated manifestation. Hegel names this manifestation "the spirit of the world."[5]

Philosophical decision is always the decision of the identity of being and thought, however it might be accentuated or modalized. This decision orders the entire history of philosophy. Indeed, it is owing to this decision that there is history: distension and passage, repeated events of the *making* and the *making itself of itself* of this identification. History is the succession of the ruptures of history where this identification plunges back in itself and decision recurs. This does not mean that decision alone reigns eternal, like the inalterable constraint of a monstrous enigma of sense. It is merely a contingent posture of thought and of history. But this means that it can be changed, this decision, only at the term of the work it engages in: there where the time for naming this identity, or for choosing to care for it, has come and gone, because it *makes itself of itself*. And this takes place in each point of truth and in each point where history ruptures.

Philosophical decision is the decision not to settle for the manifest, and this in the name of manifestation itself. This decision is the decision not to entrust the manifest to something else: to something occult, hidden, or secret. It is the decision of a world without secret, or a world whose whole secret lies in its *logos* or its revelation.

It is difficult to hold to this decision, because it is so unsettling. What is unsettling is that the negative of manifestation should turn out to be nothing hidden or nonmanifest. The laziness and repose of thought is always to give itself over to some nonmanifest thing, to which one will lend, depending on the occasion, the pomp of the most spectacular figures and ornaments, the imposing glimmer of cults or arts, the prestige of names or powers, and even the enthusiasm or elevation of great thoughts.

But the greatness of Thought is in the simplicity of the decision that turns itself toward naked manifestation. If manifestation is only what it is, if "what has been revealed is only this: that God is revealable,"[6] then manifestation is what reverts to nothing but itself. It is thus itself the entire exposition, not only of itself, but—before and after all—of what there is of *self* "itself." *Self* is precisely what reverts to nothing else: not as a pure given and independent subsistence (substance), for such a thing does not yet revert to itself, does not turn upon itself in being simply what it is. Manifestation, to the contrary, *makes a return* and is nothing but this return. But, because this return does not come to a presupposed substance, it is return to nothing—or it is not a return, and it only comes back to itself in throwing itself forth, at the surface, of which it will have been neither the underside nor the prerequisite ground—being thrown out of self as self, *being* this throw itself, and thereby its *own* passage into the other.

Thus "I = I" means nothing, or only this: passage and leap into the other of what was never in itself. This leap is unsettling twice over: in the agitation of its movement, where there is no continuity that would not also be the laceration of a burst of light,[7] and in the nonknowing of the other that thus makes up all of self-knowing.

Trembling

Thought must take the self out of itself; it must extract it from its simple being-in-itself: thought is itself such an extraction, along with the speech in which thinking takes itself out of itself and exposes itself.

The compact density of simple subsistence must be shattered, whether it be the density of stone, the ego, the whole, God, or signification. Subsistence that presents itself as a first principle, or as a starting point, is already in fact only a deposit of manifestation on the move: a deposit in being, repose in thought. To dissolve this deposit and awaken this repose are the task of thought, because it is thus that it penetrates movement.

On the one hand, this shattering of compactness is already active in compactness: it inhabits it, works it over, unsettles it *in itself*. On the other hand, the resolution of the opposition between the compact and its shattering does not occur in the transition to—or in the return to—pure movement, as to a universality itself abstract, separated, simple, and, in its turn, compact in its generality. Rather, this resolution is operated in penetrating being-closed-on-itself with its own division *for itself*: being itself in its singularity finds itself shattered or dissolved, back in movement and awakened.

The separation that is in itself manifestation is each time a singular ordeal. As such, it is pain. Pain—or misfortune—is not universal separation; it is not the pain of a great cosmic drama that sweeps every being up into it, and in which, ultimately, a universal subject would get enjoyment from universal misfortune. Pain is precisely the element of the singularity of separation because it is to singularity and as singularity that pain arises. It occurs as the alteration of its subsistence, and thus as its self awakened in its alterity.

Besides, pleasure and pain are themselves both of the other and in the other. But misfortune and joy are not one thing, although together they are the awakening of the other in itself, of self by the other. Their opposition is itself division of the other as other. To be in itself affected by the other for itself—this cannot be indifferent, or else this affection would remain simply a nuance of subsistence. The division between misfortune and joy is itself a pain. One could say: pain opens, joy reconciles. But reconciliation is in the point, or in passage. Misfortune insists, tearing the ground apart; joy throws itself out beyond itself.

To undergo pain is therefore to feel oneself singular ("The higher a nature, the more pain it feels").[1] In a general way, to sense or to resent is to find oneself sentient. But because sentience has no generality, being-affected is a determinate relation to the other—pain or joy, and this determination is also its own singularization. In misfortune, I am precisely subject, sense of myself.[2] Which does not imply compensation, nor a sublimation. And this is the case even if joy is also a "resenting"—but, according to the above-mentioned division, pain does not transform itself into joy. Right at misfortune, right at my misfortune, I recognize myself separated and finite, shut in, reduced or reducible to the very point of my pain. To know oneself as such a one is not an abstract knowledge; it is to be, concretely, before the insufficiency and incompletion of self and, by this very lack, to be in relation to the other, to all of the other and all the others that I lack: it is to be already in movement, to become. It is to become infinitely, all the way to death and to joy, which is to say, always to the point of what cannot be a result, but is passage itself.

It is thus that the subject is, and is nothing other than the act of going into movement as the movement of this being-affected and this passing-into-the-other: "A being which is capable of containing and enduring its own contradiction is a *subject*; this constitutes its infinitude."[3] The infinity of the subject does not float above it, nor is it a kind of inconsistent flux that would come out of it. Nor is it a kind of sublime or heroic overcoming of misfortune, through which the subject would keep itself up above itself as above a tragic spectacle. In this sense, my infinity is also not in my death, as in a "non-actuality"[4] where precisely I no longer am. But my death is in my singularity in itself and for itself affected by the other. "Death" is what there is of the other (the death of the other, therefore, as much as mine), and thus is the infinite actualized for me.

The subject does not reappropriate its other and its contradiction: that it knows this contradiction to be its own, and that this knowing is exactly what constitutes it as subject, does not make its own contradiction become its subsistence. It remains its contradiction, just as my pain, my death, and my other, or my joy, remain outside of me: outside of me—what, being *mine,* makes me go out of myself. It is what, in me, negates me as me; what negates my determination, and what precisely relates it to the other—which is to say, what also relates this determination to itself, opening it in itself for itself.

Self-knowing in negativity and as negativity is therefore no more a knowing than it is a victory that would subdue or domesticate pain, death, the other, or joy. It is not knowing of an object; it is self-knowing—but only to the extent that, in this knowing, self does not become its own object. It is the subject, and the subject is self-knowing. And its self-knowing is its negativity relating itself to itself, for itself. The subject is—or makes up—the experience of its being-affected as the ordeal of what dissolves its subsistence. But again: it is not "some thing" (pain, death, the other, or joy) that undoes this subsistence from the exterior. It is not another subsistence that divides the subject; it is substance that divides itself—that enters into relation, or that opens itself to it, or that manifests itself. The subject is the experience of the power of division, of ex-position or abandonment of self.

"Self" "is" only this: negating itself as in-itself. Self in itself is nothing, is immediately its own nothingness. Self is only fissure and fold, return upon self, departure from self, and coming to self. That is why the Hegelian "self" has its concept only in the multiple and infinite syntax of these expressions: *in itself, for itself, right at itself*, or *near itself, unto itself, outside of itself*. Self is selfsame: the position of this sameness engages that of a difference, whose movement alone posits sameness. Self is *as* itself; which is to say, at the same time, self *as such* and *like* itself. In order to be in truth, and to have or to make sense, self must be self as such: and it must be so in taking distance from itself in order to posit itself as something like what it is.

One might here be tempted to object that this moment of resemblance—and thus of alterity and exteriority—gets erased because this resemblance is resemblance to self rather than to the other. One might then think that a general mimetics would be more appropriate than the thought of the process of making-itself-selfsame. But what makes itself either way is still identification.

Hegel is not unaware of the moment of identification. This moment belongs to the very first determinations of the subject that senses itself, and that senses itself in the other and as the other (imitation, but also immediate communication and "magnetism").[5] It is the immediacy of identification that then develops for itself. And this immediacy, from the outset, inscribes "in" the self the moment of its passivity: the moment of this passivity whereby the act of making itself self only comes out of a making itself (or being made) like the other.

In its very first figure, this relation to the other, and, more precisely, this being-self-through-the-other, gives itself as that by which "substance . . . is made to tremble."[6] It is with this trembling that the mother's "self" affects in herself, and awakens, the child—which so far is in her womb only as a substance—as an identity that has its own being outside itself. At the other extreme, it is also in trembling that consciousness envisages death: "For this consciousness has been fearful, not of this or that particular thing or just at odd moments, but its whole being has been seized with dread.... In that experience it has been quite unmanned, has trembled in every fiber of its being, and everything solid and stable has been shaken to its foundations."[7] And in yet the same way, it is a trembling that grips "the heart when Love draws near / As though 'twere Death."[8]

We could register in Hegel a whole series of tremblings—religious or aesthetic, for example. It is always the trembling of the finite seized by the infinite: it is the sensibility of the infinite in the finite. We would also have to notice that Hegel does not properly give the concept of this image. It comes to him in those places where categories fail and themselves tremble.

Trembling is the act of being-affected—a passive acting that merely makes the body vibrate, that unsettles substance. The self trembles at being touched, awakened, roused; it trembles as much at the feeling of its fragility as in the desire for its freedom. Its emotion is its own, and its trembling is a trembling *of itself* because it is thus that it comes to itself—thus that it comes and it goes away, that it comes in the same way as it goes: trembling.

Trembling is like the unity of pain and joy—like a unity that would not be a unity and could in no way be one, and that would be one, would resemble *itself*, only to the extent that it would only be vibration differing from itself. The self has its unity in trembling of itself.

This is not merely an image, and it is not merely something like a primitive and exterior level of the self-sensing-itself—just as birth, religion, art, love, and death are not anything inferior or primitive. For "thought too... is sensed, especially in the head, in the brain, in general in the system of sensibility."[9] Thought does not only tremble before what it has to think; it trembles in itself, at being in itself detachment from self, the awakening of the other, of its pain and its joy.

Negativity makes all determinateness tremble, all being-all-to-itself: it injects it with a shudder and an unsettling agitation. What is so unsettling is the freeing of this determinateness for what it is not—for the other and for the infinite—and whose very being is already in itself the essential sharing.

If the thought of the subject thus gets characterized as an emotion, this is not the effect of thought being emotive, nor is it the feature of a sentimental philosophy. Feeling is not made originary, nor is emotion. Nor is a cold intelligence that is master of itself made to figure at the origin. In the famous "dialectic of master and slave,"[10] the mastery of the master remains an abstraction precisely insofar as the master himself does not tremble in the imminence of death. But the slave is just as much the one who trembles before the master. Their struggle is that of the consciousness that exposes itself of itself to its own desire to be recognized and to be desired by the other: but the other as such, and as the other self subsisting outside of me, imperils my subsistence, this being-all-to-myself that I thus know can only be affirmed in risking it. I cannot stop trembling before the other, and even further, at being in myself the trembling that the other stirs up. And thought cannot penetrate the thing without trembling.

Sense

Sense is a "wondrous" word that designates "the organs of immediate apprehension" as well as "the sense, the thought, the universal underlying the thing."[1] The two senses of the word must
then have, in their distinction and in the opposition that this
distinction presents, the same sense. The sense of the word *sense*
is thus in the passage of each one of the two significations into
the other. This passage itself will not allow itself to be grasped as
a third independent signification. There is nothing more, in its
"wonder" (*wunderbar,* "stunning, surprising, uncommon"), than
an interesting and pleasant contingency of language: as if language, at one point, let be instantaneously glimpsed the incessant transport between significations that structures it and that
mobilizes it through and through. Language does not determine
this transport any further than as the instability and the fragility
of an encounter, of a division, the unity of which cannot be ar-
rested or pinned down. It makes sensed an "at the same time"
that is nothing more than the evanescence of a slight linguistic
discrepancy.

But what thus makes itself sensed gives itself to thought. Sensibility and ideality are one through the other, one for the other,
and one in the other. In sensibility, being-for-itself awakens: it
differentiates itself from the simple being-right-at-itself in which
it is still asleep. The "right-at-itself"—which already bears the
fold of self upon self, identity stuck on itself—unfolds or unglues

its own adherence. Upon awakening, I am an other. There are things outside me, and I myself am for myself the one who has these things in front of him.[2] Doubtless, the sentient being that is only sentient also becomes its own sensation and sinks into it: but, *in and as* sensation, such a being also becomes what it is as its subject. Sensibility is becoming: passage from a simple determinateness to a property. Sensation is mine—or rather, if it is not yet the universal mineness of the one who says "I," it is, in animal and vegetal sensation, the sensation proper to one who senses.

This property or this appropriation as such is an ideality: because the proper is the position of one separated off as "its own," and is therefore also the position of a thing separated off as an other's own self, to the very extent that this other in itself is already its own. The proper, as such, is not a possession or a dependent of a given subject. The proper takes place as appropriation, which is to say, in the "union of [the person] with himself"[3] that characterizes "propriety" in the juridical sense; and the proper is thus not a given, but the relation of coming to self. Nothing is properly proper without being incessantly reappropriated, taken and thrown back into this relation. (In this sense, the proper is the negation of the exteriority of possession and of its fixation in the abstraction of the right to own property.)[4] The proper is therefore not a thing, but always the sense of a thing: just the thing— as one says of a tool appropriate to a task—with its truth in an other. Appropriation makes it that something does not simply become dependent on me, but enters for me into my independence, into the sphere of my action and of my personality. The proper is what came into an other as it came into its self—much as the proper meaning of a word is its way of giving, through its definition in other words, what only it is supposed to say to the exclusion of every other word.

As appropriation, sensibility divides a subject and its other, making the other come about for the subject, and makes the subject for itself in what becomes *its* other. The other pure and simple, the other merely juxtaposed to the other as well as to the same, is not yet an *other*: it is an in-itself next to an in-itself, just alike. The truth of the other is, to the contrary, to be *my* other, irreversible and unexchangeable, even though I am in my turn *its* other and just as irreversible. And it is thus that my truth is to become for myself in my other. To be for self, to exit simple being-other—such is ideality.[5] Sensibility therefore passes of itself into ideality, and the first sense of "sense" passes into the second. Still more precisely: sensibility is not only the particular quality of organized beings, but it is also what of itself has sense, the sense of passing into the ideality of the proper.

(Actually, there is something of sense that also precedes the sensibility of beings with sense organs. The inorganic is not sensitive in the active sense, but it is the sensible matter that is sensed in every sensation—for every sensation plays itself out right at matter, which is to say, right at an alterity that is in itself without self. The inorganic is in itself individuality "without intrinsic form"[6] or what itself negates itself as self. The stone has properties, but it has them purely outside itself. They are qualities, posited one next to the other. They are the simple negativity of the proper, and only appropriable for an other—attainable, edible, transformable, consumable by the other. Thus, matter—that is to say, the "sensible"—exposes not a pure absence of sense, but the unbinding of sense and sensible exteriority, offered up to the appropriation of a sensation or an ideation.)

Ideality, being the for-itself considered as such, is thus present right at sensibility itself: strictly speaking, the for-itself is always already present right at the in-itself, and this presence is not some other thing than the movement, albeit latent or inchoate, of manifestation. In ideality, or as ideality, the thing becomes for itself, or becomes all by itself: it is unto itself collection and shelter of its being. It is not simply given there, but it is pre-sented (or pre-sensed); and, from this fact it gets, or rather, it is a form.

According to the most ancient (i.e., Platonic) determination of the concept, the Hegelian idea indeed designates form. Form is not the exterior of a thing, superimposed on its interior content. The form is that by which the content presents itself, and because its presentation is not foreign to it, because it is its manifestation, the form is much rather this: *that* the thing manifests *itself*. The form is the content revealing itself.[7]

The idea—which is the proper concern of thought—is the power of appropriating form. Its necessity and its operation are "to seem and to appear."[8] The idea is not an idea "of" the thing (and even less "about" it), nor is it the ideal thing ("merely thought"); it is the thing itself forming itself in its manifestation. In ideality, considered as the separate regime of intellection, of representation and formal conception, what gets isolated is the revelatory moment of manifestation. In sensibility, considered as the separate regime of immediate and nonexplicitated appropriation, what gets isolated is the revealed moment of manifestation. But ideality is ideality *of* sensibility, and sensibility is sensibility of ideality: otherwise, these very notions make no sense. The revealed and the revealing can only be together in revelation, and it is thus that there is *sense* in general: that there is presence for itself. And it is thus that Hegel can say that "everything is in sensation."[9]

Sense is the ideality of the sensible and the sensibility of the idea: it is the passage of the one in the other. Sense is thus total and infinite; it is the infinite relation to self of everything, the whole as such—which is to say, the relation to self of each and every thing, one through the other, for the other, in and as the other. And the most general form of this total relation, represented in its greatest distension, is the relation between the thing in itself (inert desposited being, obscure block not even present) and the thing for itself (the idea forming itself, the turning concept closed on itself).

But purely impenetrable thickness and the idea purely penetrated by itself are two abstractions—two extremities of separating abstraction, and something like the face-to-face of stupidity and madness, and the utter loss of sense. To the degree that thought is separation, it cannot avoid not only designating, but brushing up against, these two extremities.[10] Sense passes between the two, from the one to the other absence of sense, from the one to the other truth.

If truth is sense, it is not as the "reasonable" middle ground between these extremes. It is sense as their mediation, which is not a middle term, but the means or the middle itself as the passage of one extreme into the other.[11] This passage is the penetration into the other, and sense is in mediation. And because mediation is the passage of the in-itself to the for-itself, and vice versa, mediation does not subsist by itself as a third term in which sense would deposit itself, but it is sense insofar as it dissolves itself in its operation.

Sense is therefore what makes itself sensed and what gives itself form in passage and as passage. This does not mean that sense is an evanescent breath, a fugitive scintillation. It cannot be fixed upon; it is nonfixity itself. But this means that it is incessant movement and activity: as much the perpetual movement of significations in language as the movement of history in which nature and man never cease passing—in the double sense of this word: being-in-passing, and passing away—and as the movement of acting, of human operation and conduct, which have to free, always anew, the truth of sense for itself.

That sense is total and infinite, that it is the appropriating event of all things in thinking penetration and in effective passage, this absolutely does not mean that sense would be given with what is, as it is. Totally to the contrary: nothing is, just as it is, in sense. Necessary to sense are the activity of becoming, and manifestation. Sense is not "the meaning of being," as if it were a given property of being, or an ideal signification floating above it, more or less perceptible to the minds of men. Sense is being as sense, being torn away from subsistence and away from fixed determination; and it is the appropriation of being by the subject, as subject. The restlessness of the negative is the agitation, the tension, the pain, and the joy of this appropriation.

This is why the decisive concept at the heart of mediation—the one Hegel declares to be "one of the most important concepts of philosophy"[12]—is designated by a term that presents, like *Sinn* and a few others, but in the most dynamic form, the remarkable property of conjoining two opposite senses, and of thus being by itself, in itself, and ultimately upon itself, the operation of the mediation of sense in general.

The word in question is *Aufhebung,* which in German can designate both the action of suppression, of making cease (which is the usual sense), and that of gathering or retaining something. *Aufhebung* is the suppression that conserves. It conserves the thing in raising it to the idea: what is *aufgehoben* is the same thing as the ideal *[idéel].* In French, one will choose to say that the thing is *relevée.*[13]

The word *Aufhebung* permits, by happy chance, of playing out right on this word the conjoined suppression of its two possible significations, the sublation or up-heaval of the one by the other. In short, this word offers the exact counterpoint to the word *Sinn,* which permits of playing out the simultaneous presentation of its two significations. The sense of up-heaval is the upheaval of sense; or one might say, more playfully, that the sense of upheaval takes leave of sense or takes up where sense leaves off.[14] This play is only the pleasant side, in itself insignificant, of the movement whose other side is the most serious penetration of thought.

The concept of sublation is the concept of that which is its own upheaval and which, because it itself suppresses itself, itself succeeds itself, takes up where it itself leaves off. It is the concept of dialectical mediation, which is nothing other than manifestation considered according to the form of its operation. Insofar as it is relation to self, manifestation is mediation. Manifestation is precisely mediation between the thing and itself—between the sensible and the ideal of the same thing. It consists neither in passage through a medium nor in the intervention of a mediating third term. It is simply the step out of the in-itself: self is relieved of its function of being in-itself. Being does not remain in itself: it liberates itself.

The mediating *Aufhebung* is therefore not at all a mysterious power, and the dialectic is not an obscure machination of nature and history. Actually, the dialectic is only an operation, and sublation is only this strange autosuppressive category, to the extent that one isolates in analysis the formal or operative moment. But, for itself, mediation should not be isolated, nor can it be. To think mediation is to think the impossibility of keeping determinacies isolated. It is not to leave off at the given, in order eventually to provide the given a sense that is itself determined. It is, on the contrary, to penetrate revelation: that the given *always gives itself as something other than simply given.* This way of "giving itself" is mediation—and this mediation is therefore that of being itself, and not exterior to it. What is thus "of being"—proper to being itself—is to negate itself as being so as to become sense. In becoming sense, being does not suppress itself in the way that one destroys some thing. It denies being the being of impenetrable subsistence, and in this negation it affirms being the being of sense.

This affirmative negation—sublating negation itself—being does not pronounce it or operate it from out of an extant position. This negation is the *Faktum* of being, and it comes entirely out of being. Mediation: we cannot pronounce it at a distance, as one would enunciate a law of things. We cannot because we are ourselves in it. But we are not in it as we would be at the heart of an environing reality. We are in it as we are in our own determination as thinking beings—which is to say, beings for whom negativity presents itself as such and for itself: in us it is said that being is not simply being.

What thus gets said could therefore never merely be said—and that is why it exceeds the possibilities of nomination. What is not merely said is what is effectively done. The mediation and the sublation of sense, or in sense, is what we have to do—that is our most proper concern, our every instant's responsibility, and the effectivity of our history.

In the history of philosophy, the "dialectic" has always been the name of diverse ways of making sense—of making the *logos* play or work—there where no first or last signification is given. For Plato, Aristotle, or Kant (granted considerable differences), this condition was restrictive, or negative. Hegel makes of it the very condition of truth: that it not be a given.

For this reason, the discourse of philosophy can only be the discourse of negativity for the sake of negativity itself. It ceaselessly enunciates the negation of determination. Its whole syntax is the indefinite amplification of the proposition: A = not-A and I = not-I. Its whole semantics consists in sublating each signification of A or I into another, then into the negation of every signification.

This is also the reason why philosophy knows itself to be "gray" insofar as it is the discourse of the concept, in the usual sense of the term: in the sense of the "notion" or the "category," which is to say, within the merely theoretical moment or function, in which the absolute concept—conception or grasp, penetration—posits itself in distinguishing itself from knowing that is only knowledge. Discourse is always "shadow" and "lifeless mist."[15] This does not mean that one can make short work of the gray shadow, where thought posits itself as such, and exposes its stakes. But this signifies that the ultimate stake is also, for philosophy, to know itself and to posit itself as negation of self: philosophy is still nothing more than the discourse—as such, separated and abstract—of the sense that exposes itself in it as negation of discourse and as passage to the act, to the praxis of sense.

But it is precisely for this reason that philosophy is what it is, and is neither art nor religion, which are the two figures of fulfilled mediation or of sense.[16] Art and religion are sense presented: which is also to say, merely presented, merely in figures. As figures—and, further, figures of figuration itself—art and religion indicate of themselves their own mediation within philosophy, for what both the one and the other represent is how representation exceeds itself. The one and the other represent this in passing one into the other: religion must fulfill itself in sensible manifestation, but this manifestation itself reveals itself as an "implicit or more explicit act of worship *(cultus),*"[17] whose truth is to depose itself and to pass beyond itself as cult. And the correlate of the cult, the divine figure, disappears with it.

Thus art and religion are different modes of truth "giving itself an existence"[18]—but they do this in such a way that this tangible existence indicates nothing other than its own passage beyond itself, or its own sublation. What is posited in art, just as in religion, is that it cannot be a matter of merely representing sense: one must enter its movement and penetrate its act. Philosophy, then, is not a representation of a higher order: it is the naked exposition of this exigency. Philosophy, therefore, is no more a negative theology than it is the prayer of reason or the poem of thought. It forms the *sublation* of the one and the other. It does not address itself to any Other, and it does not entrust itself to the splendor of any form, because it is the thought of the other at work: negativity for itself.

As thought, philosophy endlessly sublates itself in enunciating its negativity—and, as work, it sublates itself in the activity of the concrete subject that has to live and to die, alone and numerous, nature and history, and which thus makes experience of sense, or of the idea "which emancipates itself."[19]

No more than it has properly begun does discourse properly end. Or, rather, just as it began with the decision to philosophize, it interrupts itself upon this decision's becoming concrete: to live and to die sense.

Desire

The self is in itself negativity. If it is designated as "self," this is not because of any privilege accorded to identity or subjectivity. On the contrary, one could say—and by all rights—that Hegel is the first to take thought out of the realm of identity and subjectivity. But he thus fulfills the program of all of philosophy; he exposes it as such, in its most ample constraint.

"Self" means being unto the ordeal of being. Being that has nothing to found itself, to sustain itself, or to fulfill itself is being posited naked in its identity with the *logos*—it is naked substance identical to its absolute freedom—it is the naked infinity of singularities, none of which achieves the whole. In one or another of these forms—and philosophy has conceived more than a few others—the ordeal is that of immanence. Being rests in itself, and this rest itself awakens and unsettles it: at rest, it feels itself lose its sense of being. In truth, it has already lost it. The simple position of being is privation of sense, but it is as privation that sense first manifests itself. This contradictory, though imperious, condition makes up the structure and history of philosophy. All the rest is variation on this theme—exhausting and necessary variation. The theme also gets transformed in the process of variation; it even ends up, perhaps, disappearing into it. It could happen that we stop worrying ourselves with sense, either as individuals or as communities. It could even be that this always happens anew, discretely. But philosophy cannot grasp this disappearance.

It leads us rather to let ourselves be grasped by it—and, above all else, not to confuse this disappearance with an illusory, religious, or fantasmatic certainty.

"Self" therefore means sense left to its own devices, sense that makes itself sense, not by a recourse, but by an infinite return to the same, to this other-sameness that is all that offers itself. "Self" is therefore first of all what finds itself as nothingness. Rigorously: self is what *does not find itself.* Self is negation of self, negativity for itself. In this for-itself of the negative, there is no finality, no intentionality, no "in view of." There is infinite distance, the absolute difference in which self undergoes itself, and *as* which self undergoes itself. Its absolute knowing is already there, and this is why this knowing is not a science, not a belief, not a representation—but becomes. Absolute knowing passes absolutely, and this is precisely what it knows; and its passage is its knowing, and its freedom.

Thus, to the extent that the concept or grasp is "absolutely self-identical negativity,"[1] "singularity [is] a self-relation and indeterminate negativity."[2] The identity of the concept and singularity is properly the identity of the subject. It is the identity of negativity related to itself twice over: once in the idea, and once in concretion. The subject is the effectivity in-itself-for-itself of negativity, negativity right at itself and all by itself *[chez soi].* At the same time, this signifies that the grasp only actualizes itself in the here and now of the singular, just as the singular only has its truth in the penetration in itself of the negative. I know the truth outside of myself, and I know that I am the truth outside of myself. Me, the truth, I know that I cannot confuse myself with any "self."

In a sense, one would have to say that the subject is its own negation, that it is the subject that takes leave of its contingent determinateness, as well as the subject that takes leave of the abstract universal, and that it thus does nothing but posit itself, by its own power, which alone forms and works its substance. The subject would be infinite autodetermination and autoplasticity—of the whole, in and as everything. Absolute knowing would only be an immense tautology of the subject—all things considered, rather ridiculous, and menacing if used as a practical model.

But that would be to forget the essential double condition of this entire apparent tautology. On the one hand, singularity is not a wasted word: it is the concretion of separation; it is manifestation that only fulfills itself in a closed form, this or that, her or him, here and now, not otherwise nor elsewhere, between this birth and this death, unexchangeable. No generality and no universality are worth anything unto themselves, nor can they subsume or sublimate the absolute position of the singular. But, on the other hand, to say that the subject is its own negation does not restore to it any power or any subsistence other than those, precisely, of negativity. The subject does not negate itself as someone who commits suicide. It negates itself in its being; it *is* this negation, and thus does not return to itself. *Self* is precisely without return to self; *self* does not become what it already is: becoming is being outside of self—but such that this outside, this ex-position, is the very being of the subject.

This double condition, therefore, must be upheld: do not give way, either on concrete singularity (put nothing off on the heavens, the future, or some collective abstraction) or on negativity (put nothing off on an identity, a figure, or a given). One must think concrete negativity.

The concretion of negativity begins with the other. The self that negates itself, instead of coming back to itself, throws itself into the other, and wills itself as other. This is why the other is not second, does not come after. If the other, by the simple fact that I name it "other," seems to presuppose the "one" or the "same," and thus only to come later, this is the effect of a still abstract thought that has penetrated neither into the one nor into the other. The one does not begin: it begins *with* the other. With the other means near to the other, with the other at his place. I am first the guest of this other: world, body, language, and my "twin" [*mon "semblable"*]. But being the-one-with-the-other can only provisionally pass for a unity.[3] No more than the other is a self that would have, all to its self, the subsistence that I lack does this being-with-the-other form a higher subsistence, in which the one like the other would find themselves together, identical. The other posited as a consistent and given exteriority is precisely what is negated in the very movement of the negation of the self.[4]

This must be enunciated in two ways at the same time: on the one hand, the other is as much self as me and, as we know, this being-self is already there in itself right at the most simple given exteriority, there in compact matter. Consequently, the other takes leave of itself in the same movement as the one, and their being-one-with-the-other is necessarily a community of negativity. On the other hand (and this is the same thing), the self taking leave of itself does nothing other than negate all given subsistence. Out of the other as compact exteriority I make *my* other, just as *it* makes me *its* other.[5] I take the stone out of its mineral abstraction; it takes me out of my spiritual mass.

The move out of self is therefore equally the appropriation of the other. But this appropriation does not, for all that, make the other my thing—neither in the sense that, in identity with the other, I find myself subsisting in myself, nor in the sense that the other, in my identity, would be simply an object in my posses-sion. The relation with the other, precisely to the extent that it is appropriation, is appropriation of the negativity out of which this relation comes: it is dissolution of the determinateness given outside of myself because it is dissolution of my own determinate-ness, passing outside of itself. The stone becomes, for example, a tool, and I become a stonecutter.

But here again, and here above all, one must not give way on the rigor of negativity. Negativity dissolves the given-other, not in order to restore it to a self that has precisely been shattered in itself, but in order to make it a nongiven-other: to make it the other which, as *my* other, is the infinite alterity, in me, of the self itself, or what is in itself the infinite alteration of the self. My truth is not in the other so that it might be deposited in a new in itself, or in a new me, or, for that matter, in a common self.

No authoritative agency can retain or contain infinite movement—neither a particular agency, nor a general one. This is also
why thought that is only thought, and that, as such, only knows
agencies—subjects, predicates, copulas, forms of judgement and
of reasoning—remains distanced from the truth of passage. This
thought must become thought that passes itself. In penetrating
the thing, it suppresses the "merely thought pure concept,"[6] and
it enters into that recognition of the other which Hegel names
"love."

This love does not correspond to its romantic representation.
Thought does not lose itself in an effusion, nor in a generous
abandon. On the contrary, it finds in love all the precision, all the
patience, and all the acuity that penetration into effective and
active singularity demands. This singularity, as my other, is neither
an ether where thought loses itself (as in a belief) nor a thickness
in which it sinks itself (as into a feeling). Love designates the
recognition of desire by desire. One would have to say that it is
recognition of one put-out-of-itself by one put-out-of-itself—
consequently, a recognition that is not one, that is not of the "one"
by the "other," and that therefore is also not the thought of the
one about the other, but the alteration of each one.

Thus, what Hegel thinks of as love is not immediate union
represented as sentimental—although, at the same time, love is
always sentiment, which is to say, sensibility, and, more precisely,
sensitivity to sensibility itself, trembling of the other in me, which
makes me tremble and which bears my subsistence away with it.
We should go back to the poem that Hegel cites:[7]

> So trembles the heart when Love draws near
> As though 'twere Death in very deed:
> For wheresoever Love finds room,
> There the ego, sullen despot, dies.
> So let him perish in the gloom,—
> Thou to the dawn of freedom rise.

The heart trembles because the self is indeed bound to disappear, and it is this disappearance that it must want in order to be

in love, and in its freedom. But one must also consider what it means that this discourse has recourse to a poetic expression that can only seem to us sentimental or hackneyed. It means[8] that trembling must effectively come about, must come from outside to disrupt the chain of the certainties and operations of the self—including the chain of its laborious arguments on the necessity of its move out of self in itself and for itself. The poem, here, must not be taken as a poem in the sense of an artwork come to liven things up: it must be grasped as an interruption of discourse that lets there surge up the injunction or appeal of the other, as other and to the other. (Hegel introduced his citation, writing: "In order to give a clearer representation of it, I cannot refrain from quoting a few passages. . . ." It is only a representation, but its exteriority becomes, at a certain moment, necessary and, in any case, irresistible.) It is only in a breach that the self effectively abandons itself, and that negativity becomes for itself. In other words, love is what comes from the other to unseal the consistency of the self. It was therefore right to say that this unsealing, this alteration in negativity, did not come from the self. The effectivity of the self—which is to say, the death of the "despotic ego" and of being-sufficient-in-itself—effectively comes to the self from the other. And likewise, with the same effectivity, philosophy must become other than its discourse: poetry perhaps, at times and in passing, but more certainly love—desire for a knowing that itself is desire, and that only knows in desiring.

Trembling from the trembling of the other, and with the other, the self comes into desire. Self-consciousness is essentially desire, because it is consciousness *of self* as and out of its consciousness *of the other*. If self-consciousness kept itself within the immediate immobility of an "I = I," it would not even be *consciousness*. The simple position of the I is an abstraction. On the contrary, the concrete awakening of the I is its awakening to the world and by the world—the world of alterity in general. Waking up is pre-

cisely the experience of the other that arrives and that, thus, un-
covers me to myself as that *to which* or the one *to whom* the other
arrives.

The self must come from the other, and it is in this coming, as
this coming, that it has to be "self"—which is to say, unity with
itself. This necessity makes desire: "this unity must become essential to self-consciousness; i.e. self-consciousness is *Desire* in general."[9] Desire is the necessity of consciousness: it is the necessity
that the unity of consciousness come and become for consciousness itself. Desire is therefore less the tension of a lack, and the
projection of a satisfaction that would annul it, than it is the tension of the coming of the other as the becoming of the self. (When
desire satisfies itself in an immediate pleasure, it is only one side
or one moment of consciousness.)[10]

The self, insofar as it is for itself, does not have a desire or de-
sires, but is desire—which is to say that essentially it becomes
self, and that it becomes self in the other; or, if one can put it this
way, it is what becomes of the other: its own becoming is of the
other. Becoming and the other are indissociable. Becoming is the
movement of the other and in the other, and the other is the truth
of becoming. Desire is therefore not merely unhappy relation to
the other. In the unhappiness of lack, just as in the satisfaction of
possession or of consummation, there is but one isolated side to
desire. The truth of desire itself is still other: it is precisely *to be
other*, it is alterity as infinite alteration of the self that becomes.
Desire is neither aspiration nor demand, nor is it lust or voracity.
It demands nothing but the other, and is satisfied with nothing
other: but the other as such, the veritable other of the self, is not
an object one could demand, an object with which one could
take satisfaction.

This is why desire cannot become what it is in an object, in a
given determination. It is desire of the other self-consciousness.
The subject is desire of the subject, and there is no object of desire.
Desire is appropriative becoming in the other. If it is, in a sense,

appropriation *of* the other, it is of the other as other. Which means that, in appropriating the other to myself, I do just the opposite of a taking of possession or an assimilation. I do not reduce the other to the same; it is, rather, the same—the one-sided, closed-off, and "despotic" "ego"—that makes itself other.

To make itself other is also not to identify itself with the other in the sense of a fusion and a confusion of identities. We are not in the reverie of romantic love—which is, moreover, why we are in what first presents itself as a confrontation and as a struggle of consciousnesses. But what the struggle manifests is that each one has consciousness of being desire of the other because the other, being itself desire of its other, is desire of me. I desire the desire of the other: I desire that the other recognize me—and I desire that the other recognize me as the desire that I am, as the infinite becoming-self that I am.

Struggle is also the phenomenon of the very thing whose reality is love. But make no mistake. Hegel does not give us a pacifying and conciliatory vision of the hardness of human relations. The phenomenon is nothing secondary: it forms the necessity of manifestation. Love itself must manifest itself as struggle. But the struggle does not thereby lose any of the hardness in which relations of power and exploitation are engendered. Knowing that "love" is the truth of struggle[11] does not lead to preaching some stale fraternity. On the contrary, the injustice and cowardice of power must be denounced and, in their turn, negated.

But love no longer allows consciousness to fix itself upon an object, whether it be in the mode of enticement or oblation. Once the other is only an object, it is only my object, and the self is only the subject of this object—in its turn, an object for the other just as for itself. This is why, in desire, "the action of the one has the double significance of being its own action and the action of the other" and why "they *recognize* themselves as *mutually recognizing* one another."[12] The recognition of desire, in desire, is very exactly the contrary of the recognition of an object that reduces it to conditions already known and given from somewhere else. As desire, the subject does not reduce the other to itself any more than it finds itself in the other. But the subject rather becomes becoming itself, to the extent that becoming must be understood, not as a becoming-this or -that, this one or that one, but as negativity for itself.

That is what desire names: relinquishment as appropriation. But appropriation is the grasp (the "concept") of this: that the proper happens as letting go. At this point, it becomes necessary to posit that this grasp—the grasp of letting go—cannot be the doing of consciousness as such. If the strictest formulations of the dialectic often inspire perplexity, annoyance, and refusal, it is because they are obstinately understood on the level of consciousness—and, by the same token, as formulas in language, they are received as verbal acrobatics. But these formulations wish to make themselves understood on an entirely other level—or, still more exactly, they wish to make understood that they cannot be, as they are, understood by understanding, but rather demand that understanding relinquish itself.

Thought consists in passing into the element of the "speculative"—which word designates for Hegel the relation of ideality to itself insofar as it wrests itself away from every given.[13] But this does not signify that the truth of the thing comes to it from pure thought, as from its simple outside: "unity was [not] first added to the manifold of external objects by Thinking, and the linking was [not] introduced externally."[14] Speculative sense is not a higher signification, mysterious and elusive. It is the other of the sense of understanding. Thus it is sense such as it grasps itself, not in a consciousness and among its representations, but in desire itself: recognition that is not a representation, and that recognizes nothing represented.

That becoming-self comes to pass in the grasp of the letting-go-of-self is not sleight of hand, and it is not the poor equality of "I = not-I," which is just as empty and abstract as the other. It is a proposition that should only be taken for a proposition—articulation of a subject and a predicate—to the extent that its work, this long, exhausting work of discourse upon itself, leads to a proposition in the practical sense of the word: that this grasp take place in actuality, that it be an action, an experience, and a praxis.

The movement of consciousness does not have consciousness for its goal, and the experience of self-consciousness does not have self-consciousness at its outcome. Because its movement is the alteration of the desire of self, it is also the alteration of consciousness—of its unmoving point and its isolation—in desire that is recognized to be desire. Never will an ego recognize itself recognized by an alter ego, as if it were an exchange in the mirror of one and the same consciousness, or the sharing of the same representation. Such an abstract and cold operation can only take place in the abstraction of the "I = I" or the "I = not-I," which means that it does not take place. I only recognize myself recognized by the other to the extent that this recognition of the other alters me: it is desire, it is what trembles in desire.

To this extent, desire is not simple delectation of self—even though it is itself the sole content both of the ordeal and of enjoyment. Desire is *work,* which is to say, "desire held in check."[15] This does not mean that it is inhibited, nor turned away from its movement. But it is desire that really gives itself its other, or that really gives itself to its other. It is not enjoyment postponed until later, as if it were necessary to await a result, but enjoyment of the very movement that dissolves the fixity of a goal or a possession. Work "forms,"[16] says Hegel—which is to say that it elaborates the form of desire. The work, in its exterior form (a fabricated object, a formulated thought, a created existence, "the action of the singular individual and of all individuals"),[17] forms the manifestation of desire itself—and it is an infinite formation.

Which formation is not to be confused with indefinite exteriority and with the accumulation of works for themselves. If the work is work, it is precisely not to be deposited as a given, nor to subsist as a possession. Particular fixity and possession—as much as indetermination and pure community—run counter to the recognition in the other.[18] The work only matters when appropriated by desire. Any other appropriation is desire's simple and cold exclusion.

Freedom

Equality, not as the abstract equation of a subject = X in every subject, but as the effective equality of concrete singularities (absolute equality of the absolute): such is the element of sense, and desire is its liberation. The concept must enter into existence,[1] and effective existence can only be effective singularity, in which "the absolute return of the concept into itself, and at the same time the posited loss of itself," comes to pass.[2] Conception or grasp is not the subsumption of the particular under a generality; it is precisely the movement that negates the general as well as the particular (movement that therefore also negates abstract relation), in order to affirm what alone affirms itself in itself and for itself: the concrete singular, here and now, the existent as such, in the concrete relation of separation. Grasp is thus the grasping of the singular in its singularity, that is, in what is unique and unexchangeable about it, and therefore at the point where this unicity is the unicity of a desire and a recognition in the other, in all the others. The ones and the others—the ones who are all others for each other—are among themselves equals in desire.

Desire is thus the freedom of the singular insofar as the latter is grasped according to the "absolute separation of the concept," in other words, as detached from a mere "return in itself," from the simple return into self of the identical.

In the concept, everything is grasped as necessity: it is necessary that the self return to itself even as it separates itself from itself. In this respect, "self" is the name of necessity itself, and its movement is pure logic. One is therefore tempted to conclude hastily that Hegel's thought is a "panlogism," or the system of an inhuman mechanics of the absolute. But this is to forget that necessity must itself have a necessity, a sufficient reason: which, since its beginnings, is what philosophy has signified with *logos*. And this necessity of necessity is freedom.

In fact, freedom is the name for the necessity to be in itself and for itself detached from all fixity, all determination, from every given, and every property. But even more, it is the necessity to be detached, not as an independence fixed in itself, but as the movement of detachment right at the surface of every determinacy. In exposing this necessity as such, one gives it the form of a constraining logic. But one also exposes that its veritable content is "freedom and independence."[3]

The necessity of the concept and of thought in general—the necessity of the *logos*—is the form that the absolute of freedom takes in order to expose itself as such and as absolute constraint. The absolute of freedom is not, however, dissimulated beneath this form, as a secret that would be merely to come, or only located in a divine realm. Freedom consists in the necessity that form again dissolve itself of itself, and that the "content" be its own "form": the concrete, singular manifestation of self-liberation.

Freedom is therefore not given as a property or as a right. Freedom is nothing given: it is the negation of the given, including this given that would be a "free subject" defined only by determined rights and liberties. Being itself the appropriation of the subject, freedom is nothing that a subject might appropriate. If Hegel refers to Spinoza on the subject of freedom,[4] it is because he recognizes in Spinoza the thought of the only true freedom in the absolute, as distinct from the illusory freedom of men who believe themselves masters of their acts because they are unaware of the real determinations of these acts. Free will is only a moment and a figure of freedom: for in it there subsists, and even prevails, the given fixity of the subject as master of its choices. In affirming myself as free, I adhere to this position of an ego that is "master of its domain": this adherence has already deprived me of freedom.

Freedom is indeed independence, but independence from the "despotic ego" as much as from any political or domestic despot whatsoever. It is indeed autonomy, but the law it gives itself is precisely itself: it therefore gives itself the law to have no law, if it is itself, for itself, the law.

Generally speaking, the law is a "relation of universal determinations":[5] it posits, each time, that this is (in the law of physics) or should be (in the moral law) universally according to a universal condition. Thus "the law is something differentiated within itself." It is not a particularity differing from a generality; rather, the law states that *this* is a *universal* (for example, a body is heavy). Being for itself, the law is thus nothing other than being *self*: interior difference, or "the difference which is not one." This is not, however, the pure and simple absence of difference, the consistent unity of an "itself," but rather "difference in itself," and the step out of self that is the entirety of self-manifestation.

Freedom is the law or the necessity that posits the self outside of itself. It is thus the law of what first posits itself without law, whose law lies, precisely, in that positing. But this law—manifestation or mediation—cannot be represented as a law, for a (physical or moral) law is always "the stable image ... unaware of the restlessness of negativity."[6] Freedom is the position of negativity as such.

Because such a "position" is just the contrary of a being-posited, deposited as given, and because it is eminently "position" in the active sense,[7] freedom is the position ... of nothing, and the liberation ... of everything. Necessity and anarchy of the absolute.

Once again, the apparent dialectical ease should not mislead. It will have always been premature to impute sleight of hand. The Hegelian thought of freedom is the most difficult because it gathers and knots together all the aporias that intersect at the term "freedom"—and because it expends much effort showing the way to freedom from these same aporias. Freedom is par excellence the concept that consciousness or the understanding expects to be a given—whereas it must be the concept of nothing given, the very concept of the nongiven and the ungiveable. Here, thought forcefully states: you ask to have a freedom, whereas you have to become it.

This is also why the freedom of the absolute, or the absolute in and as freedom, is anything but the "absolute freedom" that Hegel deciphers in the Terror. This is the freedom that posits itself as absolute: it therefore posits its pure equality with itself as being immediately universal will, or as containing this equality with itself as pure and annulled difference of the law. It is thus foreign to the singularity and the diversity of effective existence. Under its juridical, economic, political, and moral forms, the pure "self-certainty"[8] of freedom is precisely only its ineffectivity; and, consequently, when it aspires to effectuate itself, its concrete inequality with itself is equal to the inequality of concrete subjects.

The experience of deliverance from tutelages and tyrannies that was the experience of Hegel's time immediately opens onto this other experience: that the erection of a free subject, of an absolute worth as such and in itself, is the alienation of the very movement of emancipation. Whether this subject be represented as individual or as collective, as law of the global market or of a universal morality, it simultaneously freezes both the concrete becoming of singular freedoms and their movement of becoming through each other into this abstract given. Freedom can lay down the law (in the sense of the law that has been specified), and can effectuate itself as the *sublation* of every law, only through the concrete equality of all: not as a legal equality, but as the real equality of an appropriation (each time, concretely singular) of my being-free. A being-free that cannot be concretely separated from yours, nor from ours, from a being-free-with-each-other.

Freedom is freedom-with or it is nothing, because it is neither independence, nor autonomy, nor the free will of a subject—no more than it is the independences of many juxtaposed subjects, even to imagine them without oppositions. It is rather the liberation of the subject: its taking leave of the density of being. One cannot say that the self is free, for such a *being* is in itself the negation of freedom. Freedom, to the contrary, is the negation of this negation, or negativity for itself. "The pure idea . . . is an absolute *liberation*."[9] If it is liberation, and not given freedom, it is because it liberates itself in and through its other: the movement of recognition is also the movement of liberation.

Freedom and negativity thus mutually expose one another. On the one hand, the negation of the given or of being-in-itself, in other words, its entry into becoming, into manifestation and desire, goes toward nothing other than freedom—more precisely, to *its* freedom, and still more precisely, to its *liberation*. Negation is first of all this movement of a self-liberation-from-immediate-being: negativity is from the very first nothing other than the hollowing out of being by its own liberation. And, on the other hand, liberation is nothing other than negativity for itself, for it is the negation of this simple negation that is the being held-back-in-itself of being.

The Hegelian privilege of negativity and the decisive character of the formula "negation of the negation" is thereby justified: the first negation is the position of the given, the fixity of which holds back, freezes, and annuls the movement of sense. To posit that being is in itself nothing is not to open an abyss in which speculative ideality would plunge the entirety of the real; to the contrary, it is to posit the thoroughgoing insufficiency of the self considered in itself—and even, in truth, the impossibility of considering the *self* for itself, of identifying it as a substance or subsistence, as an assurance or a certitude. The first negation is already freedom, but still only negatively indicated. If I penetrate this first truth, that neither the stone nor the ego has the value of simple being-there or of an identity (for example, my name, but also my self-image), this penetration is already liberation. And it is liberation of the grasping of this: that the *self* is not *there,* that it does not assume the form of being-given-there.

The second negation denies that the first is valid on its own: it negates pure nothingness, the abyss or lack. It is the positive liberation of becoming, of manifestation, and of desire. It is therefore self-affirmation. But as this liberating affirmation is not a return to the point of departure—to the stone or to me, which in turn was already only a derived given, a provisional deposit along the way and the fleeting instant of a presentation—it is also not a new, simple position. It is infinite negativity in and as act. I cannot say that the stone has become free just because it has moved from its position beside the path any more than I can say that I have become free just because I have recognized myself as different from my nominal or imaginary identity. Neither one nor the other has *become* free (as if freedom could be a result). But the stone in my slingshot, in the wall that I have built, or in the statue that a sculptor exhibits to us, indefinitely liberates itself from its exteriority, enters into a history and into multiple senses, and brings us along with it. The result is again a liberation—and that is what negativity means.

This result, however, is not indefiniteness as such—the "bad infinity" of an abstract circulation from one sense to another, from one usage to another, from one identification to another, which would always be in search of a final, sovereign, and total freedom (nature and history reconciled, postulated kingdom of ends). It is the infinite in and as act: liberation in the present of presence itself, and therefore the manifestation of singularity as such. There is indeed return to being: we have said that the *self* is return to self. It is indeed a matter of this stone and indeed a matter of me, of us. It is matter of nothing other than this world.

Now, "absolute liberation" signifies that return is a return to nothing given, but return to the given as that which gives *itself*—or to the "self" insofar as self is nothing other than a self-giving. Not, then, if one likes, a return to the world, but to the creation of the world. Not, then, to conclude, a "return," but the liberation once again of what infinitely liberates itself, starting from nothing.

The ultimate signification of negativity as freedom—or of "neg-ativity for itself"—is therefore still a negation: it is not a matter of hailing, celebrating, consecrating, or accepting the course of the world such as it is. And because it is also not a matter of meas-uring the world, with the edifying powerlessness of the "beauti-ful soul,"[10] against what it should be, it is once again a matter of liberating it. Thus, we will also not say that such and such a juridi-cal, social, or political regime makes us free and equal. Freedom and equality are always in opposition to the exteriority of the law.

Which means liberation can be for no freedom that would one day become its given result, that would present itself as its law and would incarnate itself in a figure. Liberation for nothing, in this sense, but therefore liberation for a death that would not be a "death without signification."

Such a death is at least, and first of all, death that does not come from the outside as another given, in order to reduce my presence to being only a given. It cannot be inflicted death, but only the death that individuality, as simply natural and immedi-ate, *gives itself [se donne].*[11] This is not a suicide; that is, this indi-viduality does not treat itself as if from outside, submitting to a foreign and abstract subject. Rather, it dies in and to the imme-diacy that is all it was as something given. This does not suppress the uncanniness *[étrangeté inquiétante]* of death: on the contrary, it is what makes it absolutely unsettling, and what provokes the fulgurant contradiction, the absolute pain of having to sojourn in this thought, of having to become in this penetration.

What is to be thought, then, is not that death has its significa-tion beyond itself, like a subsistence beyond the end of subsistence, or as a surviving relic. Such a signification would be precisely only a signification, and, appropriately enough, a signification attached to another subsistence-in-itself, which would do nothing more than replay the entire drama or process. It is to think—and this is thought itself—that the death which is not "death without signi-fication" is still death without signification, but in such a fashion that the nothingness of signification is also the appropriating movement of the proper "self," the grasping-and-penetration of the truth of sense.

This movement cannot be represented to the self—it is its own becoming, its manifestation, and its desire—and, moreover, it is in this way that the subject is not a subject of representation in general, but the subject of an infinite appropriation, and the subject of this appropriation in the other. This movement is not represented, but posited, in the other: in the most immediate manner, in mourning and in burial, the others bear witness to appropriation insofar as it is not that of self-consciousness in itself, but is a singular appropriation that falls outside of all immediate particularity.[12] In this way, death is an event: the appropriating event of the proper that is the outside-of-self; passage into the other, and absolute giving over to the other, to every other and to all the others, of that which can only be given over as passage itself. The other is the one who recognizes that my death is mine and is thus the "sojourn of spirit." Infinite recognition of this: an absolute singular desire has passed through here.

The event is therefore nothing other than the penetration into "completely free manifestation."[13] As such it is not different from the event of birth, from the creation of the world or the upsurge of the existent in general—that is, as singular. As long as we grasp it only on its formal side and presented as a truth, it is this event that is at stake as thought. But this event is therefore at stake as effective liberation each time that a simple given is refused, each time that a given death or a murder [mort donnée] is refused, each time that the "despotic ego's" law of nothingness is refused.

The return of freedom in itself—if one can still speak of return and of the in-itself—will therefore be nothing other than the return to the decision with which, each time, thought will have begun. Because the I is absolutely undetermined, it will have had to decide itself. Not in order to choose between possibilities given to the free will of its subjectivity: for this subjectivity is not, or is no more than, a one-sided abstraction, to which nothing is therefore given. But the I will have had to know itself precisely as "the infinity of subjectivity,"[1] to which nothing is given or prescribed in advance, and for which, consequently, there is no "good" or "duty" laid out beforehand. It "knows itself then as what chooses and decides," which is also to know itself infinite in and as act, and to become.

I do not therefore decide in favor of things proposed as possible, because I exist as "me" only in my decision. But the truth and the sense of free decision is this: I decide *myself,* I decide on myself; more precisely, I take leave of my universal indetermination and realize my infinity as singularity. It is not "starting out from myself" that I decide, as if I *was* free; in liberating myself, it is on myself, from out of myself, that I decide. Deciding oneself, liberating oneself, and giving oneself are one and the same: the self outside itself in the blossoming, the supreme manifestation of manifestation in general.

I will not have known "beforehand" what I was choosing, because there was no beforehand. But, in deciding, each time, I decide on my singularity itself that knows itself to be decisive. Either this self-knowing posits itself as "pure identity with immediate self" and thereby as subjective "interest"—which is what the word *evil* designates—or this self-knowing posits itself as this very deciding identity that does not retain itself in itself, that is thus not pure identity, but decision of self as other—this is what the word *good* designates. But this "good" cannot be designated as given, present, and qualified. The decisive subject, who is only a subject in the act of deciding, decides, as undetermined, either for the pure determinacy of "I = I," or for the infinite determination of the "I = becoming-other."

The freedom of decision is the very thing that thought, in order to begin or end, has to penetrate. But since it cannot merely penetrate it "in thought," it is not enough to have decided to philosophize in order to have penetrated the truth of decision, which is only its concrete act. So too the decision to philosophize leads only to exposing what is at stake in the form of the act—and also to exposing that this form itself is nothing yet without its effectuation as content. One could say, summarily, that everything that can be formally exposed reduces itself to this: the decision is made between the self and the other. But only on the condition of adding: this means, between the given immediate and the non-given infinite. On the one hand, consequently, the self grasps itself, knows itself, and affirms itself as the whole content of its decision. On the other hand, it decides itself for the infinite recognition of and in the other. But it does not know this, for this is not a knowledge in its possession, and it cannot, nor should it, know itself as "good"—unless it relapses into a given identity, and into a moral imaginary.

Decision is the act of concrete singularity, and the becoming of liberation. Its knowing is only absolute knowing: absolutely concrete knowing, of everyone and no one, that absolutely negates the independence and consistency of all self-certainty. Knowing of restlessness, knowing without rest—but thus, and not otherwise, *knowing*.

We

This knowing is not a knowing that would remain that of the absolute in itself and for itself. It is not the knowing of the subject, as if the subject were the absolute other, the Self contemplating itself in itself in its pure logic, its pure becoming, and its pure decision, forever returning to itself from all exteriorization and from all alienation.

Hegel has often been read as if he exhibited the autodevelopment of an anonymous Subject or Reason, foreign to us, the big Other of an autistic Self that, morever, would only be the fantasmatic correlate of the subject of a proprietary and securitary individualism: two subjects each the mirror for the other, each one as stupid and wretched as the other.

But the *truth* of a self-knowing that must be the knowing of manifestation, of the desire of the other, and of decision cannot be a truth that simply returns to itself. Truth must itself be the manifestation, the desire, and the becoming of truth—or its sense. And in this way, truth comes back to us. It finds or happens upon itself *as us,* and it is *to us* that it is entrusted.

"We" means two things:

1. The knowing that is "for us" is knowing that is not merely "for consciousness."[1] Consciousness is indeed only the knowledge of objects, and as self-consciousness, it still has the self as an object, as its other that remains its correlate. The knowing of the truth of this other as the truth of the passage-out-of-self is the knowing

for us of what consciousness, as consciousness, is unaware of in its own experience. *For us* there is sense and truth of what remains for consciousness representation and isolated signification.

But who is *we?* It seems first of all that this is us, right here, with Hegel, in the exercise of the work of thought. "We," then, seems to designate the philosopher, or those who have understood the lesson of philosophy, a more refined consciousness and knowledge that would grasp what escapes common consciousness. This appearance must be dispelled if thought is not to remain pure thought.

Without a doubt, it is correct to say that consciousness, in the movement of its experience, does not present to itself the knowing of this movement as a separate and distinct knowledge. It is, however, no less correct to say that what absolute knowing knows is nothing other than the "movement of birth and passing away."[2] It is knowing of passage, not as passage of an object, but as that of the subject itself: it is this passage itself, and knowing "for us" is essentially *the same* as that of common consciousness. And this latter, in its turn, is nothing other than the manifestation and becoming of the former.

Consequently, "we" designates neither a corporation of philosophers nor the point of view of a more elevated knowledge—and this, quite precisely, because this "we" *is us,* us all. If the moment of philosophy—of the knowing, the work, and the patience that are proper to it—must initially posit itself as a separate knowledge, as an abstract discipline of thought and as a book difficult to read, a book one will have to reread or whose reading will have to be effaced in order to penetrate the sense[3] (but whose rereading, as a separate act, is never not indispensable to the experience of truth)—if this separation is therefore necessary, it is only so as to expose this: that it is indeed a matter of *us,* and that the truth or sense staged before us as "philosophy" only has sense and truth for us.

Not that philosophy is enlisted to give them to us: for, under these conditions, truth and sense would only be something given to us, with which we have nothing to do. But they are for us, for us all—that is, they have sense and truth only in us, in our concrete existences, and only to the extent that these existences are not separate individuals, but the sharing of singularities in movement, becoming, desire, and decision.

2. "We" is defined by this: "the absolute ... from the beginning, is and wants to be in itself and for itself near to us."[4] The total movement of the "self" in-right-at-near-to-for-itself [en-à-même-auprès-de-pour-soi] would have no sense if this movement was not that of this proximity with us. "Near" (or chez) signifies that among us it is not simply in-and-for-itself that this comes to pass: neither in the in-and-for-itself of the individual, nor in that of an all-encompassing Power of the world. Neither nature nor history, neither capital nor technology is capable of being such a power; nor can the gods be other powers that would save us from the first. Rather, all of these figures expose us, through their determinateness, to the unbinding or dislocation of every "Self," of all self-certainty. It is we who are exposed, and it is therefore to us that we are exposed.

To us: to the upsurge of our existences, together, as the surging up of sense. To the upsurge of this, that the world is precisely what does not remain an inert weight, but what manifests itself as a restlessness. This restlessness is not only ours, it is itself "us"— that is, it is the singularity of singularities as such.

"We" is not something—neither object nor self—that the absolute would be near, as if the absolute were itself another thing or another self. On the contrary: that the absolute be or wants to be near us means that it is our "near us," our just-between-us [entre-nous], the just-between-us of our manifestation, our becoming, and our desire.

The absolute is between us. It is there in itself and for itself, and, one might say, the self itself is between us. But "the self itself is unrest":[5] between us, nothing can be at rest, nothing is assured of presence or of being—and we pass each after the others as much as each into the others. Each with the others, each near the others: the *near* of the absolute is nothing other than our *near* each other.

We never stop losing the "fixity of self-positing."[6] And this un-rest that *we are* and that we desire (even as consciousness be-lieves it only wants its self and its objects) is where the proximity of the absolute finds, or happens upon, itself: neither possession, nor incorporation, but proximity as such, imminence and coin-cidence, like the beat of a rhythm.[7] So beats the passage of sense: as the interval of time, between us, in the fleeting and rhythmic awakening of a discrete recognition of existence.

Selected Texts by G. W. F. Hegel

"Thought as Effectivity" from *The Encyclopedia Logic*

"The Ego Is the Purely Indeterminate" from *The Philosophical Propaedeutic*

"God Himself Is Dead" from *Hegel: Faith and Knowledge*

"The Tremendous Power of the Negative" from *Phenomenology of Spirit*

"The Force of Spirit" from *Phenomenology of Spirit*

"The Satisfaction of Desire" from *Philosophy of Mind*

"Self-knowing Truth" from *Philosophy of Mind*

"Spirit as the Likeness of God" from *Philosophy of Mind*

"Thought Is Being" from *Philosophy of Mind*

"The Absolute Concept" from *Phenomenology of Spirit*

Thought as Effectivity

From Section 19 of the Zusätze *in* LL, *pp. 26–29*

1. The first question is: What is the object of our science? The simplest and most intelligible answer to this question is that Truth is the object of Logic. *Truth* is a noble word, and the thing is nobler still. So long as man is sound at heart and in spirit, the search for truth must awake all the enthusiasm of his nature. But immediately there steps in the objection—are *we* able to know truth? There seems to be a disproportion between finite beings such as ourselves and the truth, which is absolute: and doubts suggest themselves whether there is any bridge between the finite and the infinite. God is truth: how shall we know him? Such an understanding appears to stand in contradiction with the graces of lowliness and humility. Others who ask whether we can know the truth have a different purpose. They want to justify themselves in living on contented with their petty, finite aims. And humility of this stamp is a poor thing.

But the time is past when people asked: How shall I, a poor worm of the dust, be able to know the truth? And in its stead we find vanity and conceit: people claim, without any trouble on their part, to breathe the very atmosphere of truth. The young have been flattered into the belief that they possess a natural birthright of moral and religious truth. And, in the same strain, those of riper years are declared to be sunk, petrified, ossified in falsehood. Youth, say these teachers, sees the bright light of dawn: but the older generation lies in the slough and mire of the common day. They admit that the special sciences are something that certainly ought to be cultivated, but merely as the means to satisfy the needs of outer life. In all this it is not humility that holds back from the knowledge and study of truth, but a conviction that we are already in full possession of it. And no doubt the young carry with them the hopes of their elder compeers; on them rests the advance of the world and science. But these hopes are set upon the young, only on the condition that, instead of remaining as they are, they undertake the stern labor of the mind.

This modesty in truth-seeking has still another phase: and that is the genteel indifference to truth, as we see it in Pilate's conversation with Christ. Pilate asked "What is truth?" with the air of a man who had settled accounts with everything long ago, and concluded that nothing particularly matters—he meant much the same as Solomon when he says, "All is vanity." When it comes to this, nothing is left but self-conceit.

The knowledge of truth meets an additional obstacle in timidity. A slothful mind finds it natural to say: "Don't let it be supposed that we mean to be earnest with our philosophy. We shall be glad inter alia to study Logic: but Logic must be sure to leave us as we were before." People have a feeling that, if thinking passes the ordinary range of our ideas and impressions, it cannot but be on the evil road. They seem to be trusting themselves to a sea on which they will be tossed to and fro by the waves of thought, till at length they again reach the sandbank of this temporal scene, as utterly poor as when they left it. What comes of such a view, we see in the world. It is possible within these limits to gain varied information and many accomplishments, to become a master of official routine, and to be trained for special purposes. But it is quite another thing to educate the spirit for the higher life and to devote our energies to its service. In our own day it may be hoped that a longing for something better has sprung up among the young, so that they will not be contented with the mere straw of outer knowledge.

2. It is universally agreed that thought is the object of Logic. But of thought our estimate may be very mean, or it may be very high. On the one hand, people say: "It is *only* a thought." In their view, thought is subjective, arbitrary, and accidental—distinguished from the thing itself, from the true and the real. On the other hand, a very high estimate may be formed of thought when thought alone is held adequate to attain the highest of all things, the nature of God, of which the senses can tell us nothing. God is a spirit, it is said, and must be worshiped in spirit and in truth. But the merely felt and sensible, we admit, is not the spiritual; its heart of hearts is in thought; and only spirit can know spirit. And though it is true that spirit can demean itself as feeling and sense—as is the case in religion—the mere feeling, as a mode of consciousness, is one thing, and its contents another. Feeling, as feeling, is the general form of sensuous nature that we have in common with the brutes. This form, namely, feeling, may possibly seize and appropriate the full organic truth: but the form has no real congruity with its contents. The form of feeling is the lowest in which spiritual truth can be expressed. The world of spiritual existences, God himself, exists in proper truth, only in thought and as thought. If this is so, therefore, thought, far from being mere thought, is the highest and, in strict accuracy, the sole mode of apprehending the eternal and the absolute.

As of thought, so also of the science of thought, a very high or a very low opinion may be formed. Any man, it is supposed, can think without Logic, as he can digest without studying physiology. If he has studied Logic, he thinks afterward as he did before, perhaps more methodically, but with little alteration. If this were all, and if Logic did no more than make men acquainted with the action of thought as the faculty of comparison and classification, it would produce nothing that had not been done quite as well before. And, in point of fact, Logic hitherto had no other idea of its duty than this. Yet, to be well informed about thought, even as a mere activity of the subject-mind, is honorable and interesting for man. It is in knowing what he is and what he does that man is distinguished from the brutes. But we may take the higher estimate of thought—as what alone can get really in touch with the supreme and the true. In that case, Logic as the science of thought occupies a high ground. If the science of Logic, then, considers thought in its action and its productions (and thought being no resultless energy produces thoughts and the particular thought required), the theme of Logic is in general the supersensible world, and to deal with that theme is to dwell for a while in that world. Mathematics is concerned with the abstractions of time and space. But these are still the object of sense, although the sensible is abstract and idealized. Thought bids adieu even to this last and abstract sensible: it asserts its own native independence, renounces the field of the external and internal sense, and puts away the interests and inclinations of the individual. When Logic takes this ground, it is a higher science than we are in the habit of supposing.

3. The necessity of understanding Logic in a deeper sense than as the science of the mere form of thought is enforced by the interests of religion and politics, of law and morality. In earlier days, men meant no harm by thinking: they thought away freely and fearlessly. They thought about God, about Nature, and the State; and they felt sure that a knowledge of the truth was obtainable through thought only, and not through the senses or any random ideas or opinions. But while they so thought, the principal ordinances of life began to be seriously affected by their conclusions. Thought deprived existing institutions of their force. Constitutions fell victim to thought: religion was assailed by thought; firm religious beliefs that had always been looked upon as revelations were undermined, and in many minds the old faith was upset. The Greek philosophers, for example, became antagonists of the old religion, and destroyed its beliefs. Philosophers were accordingly banished or put to death, as revolutionists who had subverted religion and the state, two things that were inseparable. Thought, in short, made itself a power in the real world, and

exercised enormous influence. The matter ended by drawing attention to the influence of thought, and its claims were submitted to a more rigorous scrutiny, by which the world professed to find that thought arrogated too much and was unable to perform what it had undertaken. It had not—people said—learned the real being of God, of Nature, and of Mind. It had not learned what the truth was. What it had done was to overthrow religion and the state. It became urgent, therefore, to justify thought, with reference to the results it had produced: and it is this examination into the nature of thought and this justification that in recent times has constituted one of the main problems of philosophy.

The Ego Is the Purely Indeterminate

From The Philosophical Propaedeutic, *pp. 13–15*

12

. . . The *practical* Absolute Reflection, however, does elevate itself
above this entire sphere of the finite; in other words, it abandons
the sphere of the lower appetites, in which man is determined by
nature and dependent on the outside world. Finitude consists,
on the whole, in this: that something has a limit, that is, that *here
its nonbeing* is posited or that here it stops, that through this limit
it is related to an "other." Infinite Reflection, however, consists, in
this: that the Ego is no longer related to another, but is related to
itself; in other words, is its own object. This pure relation to myself is the *Ego,* the root of the Infinite Being itself. It is the perfect
abstraction from all that is finite. The Ego as such has no content
that is immediate, that is, given to it by nature, but its sole content is itself. *This pure form is, at the same time, its content: (a)*
every content given by nature is something limited: but the Ego
is unlimited; *(b)* the content given by nature is immediate: the
pure Ego, however, has no immediate content, for the reason that
the pure Ego only is by means of the complete abstraction from
everything else.

13

In the first place, the Ego is the purely indeterminate. It is able,
however, by means of reflection, to pass over from indeterminateness to determinateness, for example, to seeing, hearing, and so

on. In this determinateness it has become *non-self-identical,* but it has still remained in its indeterminateness, that is, it is able, at will, to withdraw into itself again. At this place enters the Act of Deciding, for Reflection precedes it and consists in this, that the Ego has before it several determinations indefinite as to number and yet each of these must be in one of two predicaments: it necessarily is or is not a determination of the something under consideration. The Act of Decision cancels that of Reflection, the process to and fro from one to the other, and fixes on a determinateness and makes it its own. The fundamental condition necessary to the Act of Deciding, the possibility of *making up one's mind* [of *deciding*] to do something or even of reflecting prior to the act, is the absolute indeterminateness of the Ego.

14

The Freedom of the Will is freedom in general, and all other *freedoms* are mere species thereof. When the expression "Freedom of the Will" is used, it is not meant that apart from the Will there is a force or property or faculty that possesses freedom. Just as when the omnipotence of God is spoken of, it is not understood that there are still other beings besides him who possess omnipotence. There is also civil freedom, freedom of the press, political and religious freedom. These species of freedom belong to the universal concept of Freedom insofar as it applies to special objects. Religious Freedom consists in this: that religious ideas, religious deeds, are not forced on me, that is, that there are in them only such determinations as I recognize as my own and make my own. A religion that is forced on me, or in relation to which I cannot act as a free being, is not my own, but remains alien to me. The Political Freedom of a people consists in this: that they form for themselves their own state and decide what is to be valid as the national will, and that this is done either by the whole people themselves or by those who belong to the people, and who, because every other citizen has the same rights as themselves, can be acknowledged by the people as their own.

God Himself Is Dead

From Hegel: Faith and Knowledge, *trans. W. Cerf and H. S. Harris (Albany: State University of New York Press, 1977), pp. 190–91*

But the pure concept or infinity as the abyss of nothingness in which all being is engulfed must signify the infinite grief [of the finite] purely as a moment of the supreme Idea, and no more than a moment. Formerly, the infinite grief only existed historically in the formative process of culture. It existed as the feeling that "God himself is dead," on which the religion of more recent times rests; the same feeling that Pascal expressed in, so to speak, sheerly empirical form: "la nature est telle qu'elle *marque* partout un Dieu *perdu* et dans l'homme et hors de l'homme" [Nature is such that it signifies everywhere a lost God both within and outside man.][1] By marking this feeling as a moment of the supreme Idea, the pure concept must give philosophical existence to what used to be either the moral precept that we must sacrifice empirical being *(Wesen)* or the concept of formal abstraction. Thereby it must reestablish for philosophy the Idea of absolute freedom and, along with it, the absolute Passion, the speculative Good Friday in place of the historic Good Friday. Good Friday must be speculatively reestablished in the whole truth and harshness of its godforsakenness. Because the [more] serene, less well grounded, and more individual style of the dogmatic philosophies and of the natural religions must vanish, the highest totality can and must achieve its resurrection solely from this harsh consciousness of loss, encompassing everything, and ascending in all its earnestness and out of its deepest ground to the most serene freedom of its shape.

Note

1. Blaise Pascal, *Pensées,* 441 (Paris: Brunschvicg).

The Tremendous Power of the Negative

From Phenomenology of Spirit, *pp. 18–19*

32. The *analysis* of an idea, as it used to be carried out, was, in fact, nothing else than ridding it of the form in which it had become familiar. To break up an idea into its original elements is to return to its moments, which at least do not have the form of a given idea, but rather constitute the immediate property of the self. This analysis, to be sure, only arrives at *thoughts* that are themselves familiar, fixed and inert determinations. But what is thus *separated* and nonactual is an essential moment; for it is only because the concrete does divide itself, and make itself into something nonactual, that it is self-moving. The activity of dissolution is the power and work of the *Understanding,* the most astonishing and mightiest of powers, or rather, the absolute power. The circle that remains self-enclosed and, like substance, holds its moments together, is an immediate relationship, one therefore that has nothing astonishing about it. But that an accident as such, detached from what circumscribes it, what is bound and actual only in its context with others, should attain an existence of its own and a separate freedom—this is the tremendous power of the negative; it is the energy of thought, of the pure "I." Death, if that is what we want to call this nonactuality, is of all things the most dreadful, and to hold fast what is dead requires the greatest strength. Beauty hates the understanding for asking of her what it cannot do. But the life of Spirit is not the life that shrinks from death and keeps itself untouched by devastation, but rather

the life that endures it and maintains itself in it. It wins its truth
only when, in utter dismemberment, it finds itself. It is this power,
not as something positive, which closes its eyes to the negative,
as when we say of something that it is nothing or false, and then,
having done with it, turn away and pass on to something else; on
the contrary, Spirit is this power only by looking the negative in
the face, and tarrying with it. This tarrying with the negative
is the magical power that converts it into being. This power is
identical with what we earlier called the Subject, which, by giving
determinateness an existence in its own element, supersedes abstract immediacy, that is, the immediacy that barely is, and thus
is authentic substance: that being or immediacy whose mediation is not outside of it, but that is this mediation itself.

The Force of Spirit

From Phenomenology of Spirit, *pp. 490–91*

804. Spirit, however, has shown itself to us to be neither merely the withdrawal of self-consciousness into pure inwardness nor the mere submergence of self-consciousness into substance, and the nonbeing of its [moment of] difference; but Spirit is *this movement* of the Self that empties itself of itself and sinks itself into its substance, and also, as Subject, has gone out of substance into itself, making the substance into an object and a content at the time as it cancels this difference between objectivity and content. That first reflection out of immediacy is the Subject's differentiation of itself from its substance, or the Notion's separation of itself from itself, the withdrawal into itself and the becoming of the pure "I." Because this difference is the pure act of "I = I," the Notion is the necessity and the uprising of *existence,* which has substance for its essence and subsists on its own account. But this subsistence of existence on its own account is the Notion posited in determinateness and is thus also its *immanent* movement, that of going down into the simple substance, which is Subject only as this negativity and movement. The "I" has neither to cling to itself in the *form* of *self-consciousness* as against the form of substantiality and objectivity, as if it were afraid of the externalization of itself: the force[1] of Spirit lies rather in remaining the selfsame Spirit in its externalization and, as that which is both *in itself* and *for itself,* in making its *being-for-self* no less merely a moment than its in-itself; nor is Spirit a *tertium quid* that casts

differences back into the abyss of the Absolute and declares that therein they are all the same; on the contrary, knowing is this seeming inactivity that merely contemplates how what is differentiated spontaneously moves in its own self and returns into unity.

805. In this knowing, then, Spirit has concluded the movement in which it has shaped itself, insofar as this shaping was burdened with the difference of consciousness [i.e., of the latter from its object], a difference now overcome. Spirit has won the pure element of its existence, the Notion. The content, in accordance with the *freedom* of its *being,* is the self-alienating Self, or the immediate unity of self-knowledge. The pure movement of this alienation, considered in connection with the content, constitutes the *necessity* of the content. The distinct content, as *determinate,* is in relation, is not "in itself"; it is its own restless process of superseding itself, or *negativity;* therefore, negativity or diversity, like free being, is also the Self; and in this selflike *form* in which existence is immediately thought, the content is the *Notion.* Spirit, therefore, having won the Notion, displays its existence and movement in this ether of its life and is Science. In this, the moments of its movement no longer exhibit themselves as specific *shapes of consciousness,* but—because consciousness's difference has returned into the Self—as *specific Notions* and as their organic self-grounded movement. Whereas in the phenomenology of Spirit each moment is the difference of knowledge and Truth, and is the movement in which that difference is canceled, Science, on the other hand, does not contain this difference and the canceling of it. On the contrary, because the moment has the form of the Notion, it unites the objective form of Truth and of the knowing Self in an immediate unity. The moment does not appear as this movement of passing back and forth, from consciousness or picture-thinking into self-consciousness, and conversely: on the contrary, its pure shape, freed from its appearance in consciousness, the pure Notion and its onward movement, depends solely on its pure *determinateness.* Conversely, to each abstract moment

of Science corresponds a shape of manifest Spirit as such. Just as Spirit in its existence is not richer than Science, so too it is not poorer either in content. To know the pure Notion of Science in this form of shapes of consciousness constitutes the side of their reality, in accordance with which their essence, the Notion, which is posited in them in its *simple* mediation as *thinking,* breaks asunder the moments of the mediation and exhibits itself in accordance with the inner antithesis.

Note

1. ["Power" in the English translation has been modified here to conform to Nancy's title.— *Trans.*]

The Satisfaction of Desire

From Section 427 of the Zusätze, *in*
Philosophy of Mind, *pp. 168–69*

Zusatz. The self-conscious subject knows itself to be *implicitly identical* with the external object, knows that this contains the *possibility* of the satisfaction of desire,[1] that the object is, therefore, *conformable* to the appetite and that just for this reason the latter is excited by the object. The relation of the subject to the object is therefore a necessary one. In the object, the subject beholds its own lack, its own one-sidedness, sees in it something that belongs to its own essential nature and yet is lacking in it. Self-consciousness is able to remove this contradiction because it is not [merely] being, but absolute activity; and it removes it by taking possession of the object whose independence is, so to speak, only pretended, satisfies itself by consuming it, and, because it is self-end *[Selbstzweck]*, maintains itself in this process. In this the object must perish; for here both subject and object are immediate, and the only manner in which they can be in a unity is by the negation of the immediacy, and, above all, of the immediacy of the selfless object. By the satisfaction of desire, the implicit identity of subject and object is made explicit, the one-sidedness of subjectivity and the seeming independence of the object are superseded. But the object in being destroyed by the desiring self-consciousness may seem to succumb to a completely alien power. This is, however, only apparently so. The immediate object must annul itself in accordance with its own nature, its Notion, because, in its individuality, it does not correspond to the universality of its Notion. Self-consciousness is the *manifested* Notion of the object itself. In the destruction of the object by self-consciousness, the former perishes, therefore, by the power of its own inner Notion, which, just because it is inner, seems to come to it from outside. The object is thus made explicitly subjective. But by this annulment of the object the subject, as we have already remarked, removes its own defect, its diremption into a distinctionless "I = I" and an "I" that is relation to an external object, and it gives its subjectivity objectivity no less than it makes its object subjective.

Note

1. [We have changed the English translation's "appetite" to "desire" throughout this citation — *Trans.*]

Self-knowing Truth

From Section 440 of the Zusätze, *in* Philosophy of Mind, *pp. 179–80*

Zusatz. Free mind or spirit, or mind as such, is Reason that sunders itself, on the one hand, into pure infinite form, into a limitless Knowing, and, on the other hand, into the object that is identical with that Knowing. Here, this knowing has as yet no other content than itself, but it is determined as embracing within itself all objectivity, so that the object is not anything externally related to mind or anything mind cannot grasp. Mind or spirit is thus the absolutely universal certainty of itself, free from any opposition whatsoever. Therefore, it is confident that in the world it will find its own self, that the world must be reconciled with it, that, just as Adam said of Eve that she was flesh of his flesh, so mind has to seek in the world Reason that is its own Reason. We have found Reason to be the unity of subjectivity and objectivity, of the Notion that exists for itself, and of reality. Because, therefore, mind is the absolute certainty of itself, a knowing of Reason, it is the knowledge that its object is the Notion and that the Notion is objective. Free mind or spirit thereby shows itself to be the unity of the two universal stages of development considered in the first and second main parts of the doctrine of subjective mind, namely, that of the soul, this simple spiritual substance, or of mind in its immediacy, and of consciousness or manifested mind, the self-diremption of this substance. For the determinations of free mind have, in common with those of the soul, the subjective element, and in common with those of consciousness, the objective element. The principle of free mind is to make the merely given element *[das Seiende]* in consciousness into something mental *[Seelenhaftes],* and conversely to make what is mental into an objectivity. Free mind stands, like consciousness, as one side over against the object, and is at the same time both sides and therefore, like the soul, a totality. Accordingly, whereas soul was truth only as an immediate unconscious totality, and whereas in consciousness, on the contrary, this totality was divided into the "I" and the object external to it, *free* mind or spirit, is to be cognized as *self-knowing* truth.

Spirit as the Likeness of God

From Section 441 of the Zusätze *in*
Philosophy of Mind, *pp. 181–82*

Zusatz. Free mind or spirit is, as we have seen, in conformity with its Notion perfect unity of subjectivity and objectivity, of form and content, consequently, absolute totality and therefore infinite, eternal. We have cognized it as a Knowing of Reason. Because it is this, because it has Reason for its object, it must be designated the infinite being-for-self of subjectivity. Therefore, the Notion of mind requires that in it the absolute unity of subjectivity and objectivity shall not be merely *in itself* or *implicit,* but *for itself* or *explicit,* and therefore object of our Knowing. On account of this conscious harmony prevailing between Knowing and its object, between form and content, a harmony that excludes all division and so all alteration, mind in its *truth* may be called the Eternal, as also the perfectly blessed and holy. For only that may be called holy that is imbued with Reason and knows the world of Reason. Therefore, neither external Nature nor mere feeling has a right to that name. Immediate feeling that has not been purified by rational knowing is burdened with the quality of the natural, the contingent, of self-externality and asunderness. Consequently, in the content of feeling and of natural things, infinity is present only formally, abstractly. Mind, on the contrary, in conformity with its Notion or its truth, is infinite or eternal in this concrete and real sense: that it remains absolutely self-identical in its difference. For this reason, we must designate spirit as the likeness of God,[1] the divinity of man.

Note

1. [In order to conform to Nancy's title, we have changed this last sentence from "... must declare mind to be the likeness of God." — *Trans.*]

Thought Is Being

From Section 465 of the Zusätze in
Philosophy of Mind, p. 224

Zusatz. Thinking is the third and last main stage in the development of intelligence; for in it the *immediate, implicit* unity of subjectivity and objectivity present in intuition is restored out of the opposition of these two sides in representation as a unity enriched by this opposition, hence as a unity both in essence and in actuality. The end is accordingly bent back into the beginning. Whereas, then, at the stage of representation the unity of subjectivity and objectivity effected partly by imagination and partly by mechanical memory—though in the latter I do violence to my subjectivity—still retains a subjective character, in thinking, on the other hand, this receives the form of a unity that is both subjective and objective, because it knows itself to be the *nature of the thing.* Those who have no comprehension of philosophy become speechless, it is true, when they hear the proposition that *Thought* is *Being.* Nonetheless, underlying all our actions is the presupposition of the unity of Thought and Being. It is as rational, thinking beings that we make this presupposition. But it is well to distinguish between only *being* thinkers, and *knowing* ourselves as thinkers. The former we always are in all circumstances; but the latter, on the contrary, is perfectly true only when we have risen to *pure* thinking. Pure thinking knows that it alone, and not feeling or representation, is capable of grasping the truth of things, and that the assertion of Epicurus that the truth is what is sensed must be pronounced a complete perversion of the nature of mind. Of course, thinking must not stop at abstract, formal thinking, for this breaks up the content of truth, but must always develop into concrete thinking, to a cognition that *comprehends* its object.

The Absolute Concept

From Phenomenology of Spirit, *pp. 491–92*

806. Science contains within itself this necessity of externalizing the form of the Notion, and it contains the passage of the Notion into *consciousness*. For the self-knowing Spirit, just because it grasps its Notion, is the immediate identity with itself that, in its difference, is the *certainty of immediacy*, or *sense-consciousness*— the beginning from which we started. This release of itself from the form of its Self is the supreme freedom and assurance of its self-knowledge.

807. Yet this externalization is still incomplete; it expresses the connection of its self-certainty with the object, which, just be-cause it is thus connected, has not yet won its complete freedom. The self-knowing Spirit knows not only itself but also the nega-tive of itself, or its limit: to know one's limit is to know how to sacrifice oneself. This sacrifice is the externalization in which Spirit displays the process of its becoming Spirit in the form of *free contingent happening*, intuiting its pure Self as Time outside of it, and equally its Being as Space. This last becoming of Spirit, *Nature*, is its living immediate Becoming; Nature, the externalized Spirit, is in its existence nothing but this eternal externalization of its *continuing existence* and the movement that reinstates the *Subject*.

808. But the other side of its Becoming, *History*, is a *conscious*, self-*mediating* process—Spirit emptied out into Time; but this externalization, this *kenosis*, is equally an externalization of itself; the negative is the negative of itself. This Becoming presents a

slow-moving succession of Spirits, a gallery of images, each of which, endowed with all the riches of Spirit, moves thus slowly just because the Self has to penetrate and digest this entire wealth of its substance. As its fulfillment consists in perfectly *knowing* what *it is,* in knowing its substance, this knowing is its *withdrawal into self* in which it abandons its outer existence and gives its existential shape over to recollection. Thus absorbed in itself, it is sunk in the night of its self-consciousness; but in that night its vanished outer existence is preserved, and this transformed existence—the former one, but now reborn of the Spirit's knowledge—is the new existence, a new world and a new shape of Spirit. In the immediacy of this new existence, the Spirit has to start afresh to bring itself to maturity, as if, for it, all that preceded were lost and it had learned nothing from the experience of the earlier Spirits. But recollection, the *inwardizing,* of the experience, has preserved it and is the inner being, and in fact the higher form of the substance. So, although this Spirit starts afresh and apparently from its own resources to bring itself to maturity, it is nonetheless on a higher level than where it starts. The realm of Spirits that is formed in this way in the outer world constitutes a succession in Time in which one Spirit relieved another of its charge and each took over the empire of the world from its predecessor. Their goal is the revelation of the depth of Spirit, and this is *the absolute Notion.* This revelation is, therefore, the raising up of its depth, or its *extension,* the negativity of this withdrawn "I," a negativity that is its externalization or its substance; and this revelation is also the Notion's Time, in that this externalization is in its own self externalized, and just as it is in its extension, so it is equally in its depth, in the Self. The *goal,* Absolute Knowing, or Spirit that knows itself as Spirit, has for its path the recollection of the Spirits as they are in themselves and as they accomplish the organization of their realm. Their preservation, regarded from the side of their free existence appearing in the form of contingency, is History; but regarded from the side of their [philosophically] comprehended organization, it is

the Science of Knowing in the sphere of appearance: to two together, comprehending History, form alike the inwardizing and
the Calvary of absolute Spirit, the actuality, truth, and certainty
of his throne, without which he would be lifeless and alone. Only

> from the chalice of this realm of spirits
> foams forth for him his own infinitude.[1]

Note

1. Adaptation of Schiller's *Die Freundschaft.*

Notes

Introduction

1. This quotation is lifted from p. 7 of an e-mail interview—titled "Rien que le monde" (Nothing but the world)—with the editors of the journal *Vacarme* 11 (spring 2000): 4–12; my translation. It is presented in the form of a "self-criticism," one measuring the distance between the continued research on the problem of the common and community and the mutation such work has undergone: "I myself should have a turn at self-criticism: in writing on 'community,' on 'compearance,' then on 'being-with,' I certainly think I was right to discern the importance of the motif of the 'common'... but I was wrong when I thought this under the banner of the 'political'" (6–7). This need to formalize the difference between the common and the political appears to entail a re-activation of the word *ontology:* "[T]he ontology of the common is not immediately political" (7). The complications introduced in using the term *ontology* (even out of convenience, or analogically) are considerable. It is well known, for example, that Heidegger himself dropped not only the epithet *fundamental,* but the word *ontology* altogether. In the recent *Being Singular Plural* (trans. Robert R. Richardson and Anne E. O'Byrne [Stanford, Calif.: Stanford University Press, 2000]), Nancy seems even more daring: he "ambitious[ly]" proposes a "redoing of the whole of 'first philosophy' by giving the 'singular plural' of Being as its foundation" (p. xv). (This text will be cited as *BSP* for the remainder of this Introduction.) In the last section of this Introduction, I will sketch two possible responses to this apparent derivation of the political and restoration of ontology.

2. *BSP,* p. 21.

3. Jean-Luc Nancy, *The Inoperative Community,* ed. Peter Connor (Minneapolis: University of Minnesota Press, 1991). Cited as *IO* throughout this Introduction.

4. Jean-Luc Nancy, *The Experience of Freedom,* trans. Bridget MacDonald (Stanford, Calif.: Stanford University Press, 1993), p. 78.

5. Despite the historical damage incurred by the term, I use *pure* and its modifications with reference to the strictly technical sense associated with the transcendental *style* of questioning of Kant and Husserl. Nancy would probably avoid the term both for its dubious pathos and for its resonances with whatever form of transcendental idealism. Thus *nudity:* unadorned, uncovered by accidents and modifications, yet with no interiority, being *nothing but* exposure to alteration.

6. *BSP,* p. 137.

7. Nancy's recent *BSP,* however, seems particularly invested in reengaging Husserl's very difficult but decisive theory of transcendental intersubjectivity—in particular in relation to Husserl's equally important reelaboration of a transcendental aesthetic. See pp. 30–31, 61, and especially 200–201 n. 53. In the last pages of this Introduction, I will compare once again Nancy's problematic with that of Husserl.

8. Edmund Husserl, *Cartesian Meditations: An Introduction to Phenomenology,* trans. Dorian Cairns (Boston: Kluwer Academic Publishers, 1977), pp. 89–151.

9. It is important not to be misled by the emphasis on "space" and spacing in Nancy, at least at a particular level of his discourse. Without a doubt, there is a decisive critique of the simple priority of time in the phenomenological tradition dating back to Kant. But, as Nancy shows, precisely with regard to Husserl, it is necessary to think the difference between space and time from within a more ample "together" or "with": *simul, hama.* Cf. *BSP,* pp. 60–61.

10. Emmanuel Levinas, *Time and the Other, and Additional Essays,* trans. Richard A. Cohen (Pittsburgh: Duquesne University Press, 1987), p. 39; my emphasis on *is.*

11. See §52 of *Cartesian Meditations,* where Husserl "draw[s] an instructive comparison" between these two movements of constitution.

12. The term "political technology," which Nancy employs on p. 78 of *The Experience of Freedom,* is taken from Foucault. Giorgio Agamben adds that what remains most enigmatic in Foucault's work is the "convergence" of political techniques with the other "face of power," namely, "technologies of the self." See Giorgio Agamben, *Homo Sacer,* trans. Daniel Heller-Roazen (Stanford, Calif.: Stanford University Press, 1998), pp. 5ff.

It seems that Nancy, in any case, suspects the precomprehension of "technology" implied by Foucault; in speaking of a "pure mechanics of forces" and a "dynamics of power" and opposing this conception to the Aristotelian definition of the political in terms of the "nonuseful finality" of *eu zein* (*Experience of Freedom*, p. 193 n. 11), it appears that an interpretation of technique according to an instrumentalist scheme is the primary source of Nancy's "objection."

13. In volume 1 of *Capital: A Critique of Political Economy*, trans. Ben Fowkes (New York: Vintage, 1977), Marx develops a critique of the contractual form of legal obligation by showing how, within the capitalist organization of labor, the pretense of "freely" selling one's labor power to capital (the "vampire") is given the lie from the moment the means of production are monopolized by a determined class (pp. 415–16). The reformist call Marx makes for a legal restriction of the length of the working day does not conceal the fact that this quantitative demand only prepares a revolutionary "expropriation" of the means of production (p. 929). It is nevertheless the case that the problem of the "working day" allowed Marx to touch upon what is essential: that all exploitation is a matter of time. That Marx's analysis remained on the level of discussions of the extortion of surplus value, surplus labor, the wage form, the absolute and relative forms of surplus value, and so on seems to leave open the possibility of rethinking what is ultimately implied by the critique of the labor theory of value.

14. Karl Marx, *Manifesto of the Communist Party* (Peking: Foreign Languages Press, 1965), p. 35; quoted in Michael Hardt and Antonio Negri, *Labor of Dionysus: A Critique of the State-Form* (Minneapolis: University of Minnesota Press, 1994), p. 144. The chapter titled "Communist State Theory" is an excellent critical survey of various treatments of the state-form in the Marxist-Leninist tradition, beginning with a dismissal of the "purely objectivist version of the theory of catastrophic collapse" that is tied to the theory of state monopoly capitalism (p. 142). The section heading "The Illusions of Juridical Reformism" (pp. 301ff.) gives an abridged glance at Hardt and Negri's orientation.

15. V. I. Lenin, *The State and Revolution*, trans. Robert Service (London: Penguin, 1992).

16. Louis Althusser, *Lenin and Philosophy, and Other Essays*, trans. Ben Brewster (New York: Monthly Review Press, 1971), p. 137.

17. On the secondarization of juridical reform, see Hardt and Negri, *Labor of Dionysus*, pp. 301ff.

18. Cf. the Preface to *IO*, p. xxxvii; my emphasis.

19. Nancy, *The Experience of Freedom*, p. 78.

20. In other words, there is always the open possibility of good or evil: one is originally open just to this indeterminacy. But absolute evil is precisely the nonexposure to the other, and therefore to the decision for good *or* evil. In turn, Nancy's *BSP* reformulates his critique of a certain Marxist thought of the political in these terms: "Although assuredly more radical [than Rousseau] in his demand for the dissolution of politics in all spheres of existence (which is the 'realization of philosophy'), Marx ignores that the separation between singularities overcome and suppressed in this way is not, in fact, an accidental separation imposed by 'political' authority, but rather the constitutive separation of disposition" (p. 24).

21. Preface to *IO*, pp. xxxvii–xxxviii; my emphasis on "exemplary reality," "straight away," and "possibility."

22. Geoffrey Bennington, in an illuminating discussion of Jacques Derrida's recent work on friendship, seems disquieted by a similar question: "friendship can be thought to lead to . . . community, which we might think of as a condition of its taking on a *properly political* import" ("Forever Friends," in *Interrupting Derrida* [London: Routledge, 2000], p. 113; my emphasis). Clearly, what is at stake in Derrida's (and Nancy's) work is a reevaluation of what is "properly" political. It should also be noted that the "opening" of the political already begins to be closed off the moment it comes to be determined as "friendship" or, as is the case in "The Inoperative Community," "love" and/or "mourning." But the sense of these determinations is itself transformed so much as to be barely recognizable. For Hegel, love and mourning are the essential determinations of the not yet political institution of the family.

23. Nancy, "Rien que le monde," p. 7.

24. Nancy refers to this Aristotelian precedent at least twice: the first time in the Preface to *IO*, the second time at the precise point in *The Experience of Freedom* where he is formulating a critique of the notion of "political technology." Cf. *The Experience of Freedom*, p. 193 n. 11.

25. This text is cited in "The Jurisdiction of the Hegelian Monarch," collected in Jean-Luc Nancy, *The Birth to Presence*, trans. Brian Holmes et al. (Stanford, Calif.: Stanford University Press, 1993), p. 112.

26. A longer exposition of this problem would obviously have to address the question of war, for Hegel is quite clear that the state comes into existence, and manifests its freedom effectively, only at the moment and under the threat of its erasure. Insofar as it is to appear to itself at all, the state must stage itself under the sign of its own disappearance. According to the same logic, the individual is most free in the instant

and gesture of what Hegel calls "sacrifice." In §324 of *PR*, Hegel once again presents the exact argument and language from §258, here stipulating that "war" alone can make appear the difference between civil society and the state: "It is a grave miscalculation if the state, when it requires this sacrifice [of life and property in war], is simply equated with civil society, and if its ultimate end is seen merely as *the security of the life and property of individuals [Individuen]*" (my emphasis).

27. The most respectable instance of this probably comes in the Dedication to Adorno's *Minima Moralia,* trans. E. F. N. Jephcott (London: Verso, 1978), where Hegel is said to "assign to individuation . . . an inferior status in the construction of the whole," thus opting "with serene indifference . . . for liquidation of the particular" (p. 17).

28. The explicit tie-in between love and the state should shock, because we know that the state cannot be considered without the former's absence. To recall the canonical reading of Hegel: in the *Encyclopedia* (and thus the *PR*), the sphere of "ethical life" comes to sublate—and is therefore the "truth" of—what is termed (subjective) "morality." Insofar as the field of *Sittlichkeit* being structured as the syllogism of family, civil society, and the state, the family will constitute the first of three modes of synthesis. The family's is that sphere in which spirit has a "feeling of its own unity," and this feeling is not a general passibility, but the special affect of love. But to the precise extent that love is the element in which spirit feels itself, it is the most immediate form of the latter's relation to self. Not yet "conscious of unity as law," as in the specifically rational (internal) constitution of the state, love in the family is still only "ethical life in its natural form" (*PR* §158, Addition). Because nature is, moreover, principally the being-outside-itself of spirit, any merely felt unity is already or still a separation and experience of exteriority, the sheer anticipation of actual, true, effective unity in the state. It is for this reason that "in the state [love] is no longer present." Nancy develops this reading of love as the "essence" of the state in "The Jursidiction of the Hegelian Monarch," see esp. p. 129. On "love" and the absolute "between us," see the essay in *The Inoperative Community* titled "Shattered Love" in *IO*.

29. The only explicit mention within the body of the text is found in the chapter called "Present," in which a remarkable reading of the Introduction of the *Philosophy of Right* is neverthless able to call Hegel's reference to the "ethical Idea" of the state as a "romanticism" indistinguishable from characteristics of his epoch, and opposed to rigorous philosophical exigency.

30. *IO,* pp. xxxviii–xxxix; my emphasis. I have precipitously truncated this citation for my own purposes, namely, to isolate and underline the

movement of sub- or retraction, before any determination of what is subtracted. Nancy continues: "this something, which would be the fulfilled infinite identity of community, is what I call its 'work.'"

31. Ibid., p. 15.

32. The intervention of this notion of the "instant," taken from Georges Bataille, would be crucial to a treatment of *The Inoperative Community.*

33. Which is not to say that Nancy has neglected this problem. See not only "The Jurisdiction of the Hegelian Monarch," but also the chapters titled "Politics I" and "Politics II" in *The Sense of the World,* trans. Jeffrey Librett (Minneapolis: University of Minnesota Press, 1997), pp. 88–93 and 103–17. "War, Right, Sovereignty— *Technē*," collected in *BSP,* also treats this topos extensively, but only to counsel a necessary thought of the "empty place" of sovereignty.

34. See Christopher Fynsk, Foreword to *The Inoperative Community,* p. x. For the chiasmic relation between Husserl and Heidegger, see Nancy's *BSP,* pp. 200–201 n. 53.

35. I borrow this translation of *ontos on* from Peter Fenves, *A Peculiar Fate* (Ithaca, N.Y.: Cornell University Press, 1991), p. 137.

36. This imagined "response" on the part of Hegel is inspired by a passage in *Glas* in which Derrida outlines the "principle" for a "critique of the formal *I think*" as well as a "concrete" transcendental consciousness of the Husserlian sort. The "principle": "it is impossible to 'reduce' the familial structure as a vulgar empirico-anthropological annex of transcendental intersubjectivity" (Jacques Derrida, *Glas* [Paris: Éditions Denoël/Gonthier, 1981], p. 190; my translation). For this "reduction" of the familial kernel in Husserl, see *Ideen* I §§1 and 56, and *Cartesian Meditations,* §58.

37. I thank Jeff Atteberry for recalling the importance, in Nancy, of thinking freedom together with a space that is to be "left free." Cf. Nancy, *The Experience of Freedom,* esp. pp. 33–43.

38. All of Nancy's thought of "abandonment" should be linked to the figure of the desert indexed in *The Experience of Freedom,* pp. 142–47. The desert is the place where Nancy's work begins to communicate with that of Deleuze and Guattari.

Restlessness

[In the French text, the title of this chapter is "Inquiétude" (the same word that appears in the title of the book), which corresponds to the usual French translation of *Unruhe* in Hegel. Accordingly, we have most often translated *inquiétude* as "restlessness" or "unrest," which conform to the words used to translate *Unruhe* in the published English translations of Hegel's works. It should be noted, however, that *inquiétude* also has something of an affective inflection. Nancy often deploys the term in this register; and, in those cases, we have resorted to such translations as "unease," "disquiet," "unsettled" or "unsettling," "disturbed" or "disturbing," "troubled" or "troubling." Finally, there is one place in the text where Nancy exploits the way in which *inquiétude* echoes in the expression *l'inquiétante étrangeté*, the usual French translation of *Unheimlichkeit* (cf. p. 108 of the French text). — *Trans.*]

1. *PS*, C, BB, "Spirit," B, III, p. 360.

2. Preface to *PR*, pp. 22–23.

3. *PM*, §378, *Zusatz*, p. 3; translation modified.

Becoming

1. *LL*, §17, p. 41; translation modified.

2. [Although Nancy gives *PM*, §428 as the source for this citation, it is not clear to which text he is referring. Nancy explains his method of citation in the following manner: "The genre of this essay does not allow for a philological apparatus. The references to Hegel are simply given by the section or paragraph of the work, without consideration for the edition (in addition, we will use quasi citations or allusions without reference to the texts)." — *Trans.*]

3. Here as elsewhere, it would be necessary to add: with the exception of Spinoza. But this is not the place to say anything further on this subject.

4. *SL*, II, §3, chap. 1, A, p. 530: "The Exposition of the Absolute."

5. Ibid.

6. Ibid., §2, chap. 1, A, c, p. 490.

7. Ibid., §3, chap. 2, A, p. 545; translation modified.

Penetration

1. *SL*, III, Introduction, "The Concept in General," p. 577. [The German *Grund* is translated as "ground" in the English translation, but is here sometimes rendered as "depth" in order to conform to Nancy's elaboration of the term *fond*, which is the French translation of *Grund*. — *Trans.*]

2. Ibid., Introduction, "General Concept of Logic," p. 45.

3. Mallarmé: one knows how Hegelian he was.

4. Angelus Silesius: one knows the use Heidegger made of him in *The Principle of Reason.*

5. *SL*, III, Introduction, "The Concept in General," p. 585; translation modified.

6. Ibid., "The Absolute Idea," p. 835.

Logic

1. *PS*, Preface, p. 27.
2. Ibid.
3. For example, *LL* §§163–64 and *PM,* §434.
4. *PR*, Preface, p. 22.

Present

1. Immanuel Kant, *Critique of Judgment,* trans. Werner Pluhar (Indianapolis: Hackett, 1987), §68.

2. *PR*, Preface, p. 23 (it is in the same text, and the same sense, that the "the "owl of Minerva begins its flight only with the onset of dusk"); translation slightly modified.

3. With regard to this, it is necessary to read in the *LA* everything that concerns the present time as the epoch of the concept and as "deprived of life," as well as everything that opposes the sensible richness of poetry to the "thoughts that only produce thoughts."

4. *PS*, Preface, p. 19.

Manifestation

1. G. W. F. Hegel, *Encyclopedia of the Philosophical Sciences,* Preface to the Second Edition (1827), *LL,* p. 6 (in a general way, this entire part refers to this text in particular).

2. *LL,* §27.

3. [In consultation with the author, this paragraph has been revised and differs significantly from the French text.—*Trans.*]

4. *PM,* §§463–64.

5. Ibid., §549, p. 277. [This phrase is somewhat awkwardly rendered "world-mind" in the English translation.—*Trans.*]

6. G. W. F. Hegel, *Lectures on the Philosophy of Religion,* vol. 3, *The Consummate Religion,* trans. R. F. Brown, P. C. Hodgson, and J. M. Stewart with the assistance of H. S. Harris, ed. Peter C. Hodgson (Berkeley: University of California Press, 1985), "The Ontological Proof," p. 357;

translation modified. Here we must specify that, for Hegel, this phrase also means that philosophy reveals, or lets be revealed, that the "revelation" of the three Western monotheisms has nothing to reveal other than *this*—and that revelation thus passes into thought, for which there is nothing, no further god remaining at the basis, or at the surface, of the absolute.

7. *PS*, Preface, p. 7.

Trembling

1. *PN*, §359, *Zusatz*, p. 387; translation modified.
2. *PM*, §407.
3. *PN*, §359, p. 385.
4. *PS*, Preface, p. 19.
5. *PM*, §§405 and 406.
6. Ibid., §405, p. 94.
7. *PS*, B, "Self-Consciousness," A, p. 117.
8. *PM*, §573, p. 309n: here, Hegel cites a poem by Jelaluddin Rumi, a thirteenth-century Persian Muslim mystic.
9. Ibid., §401, *Zusatz*, p. 85; translation modified.
10. *PS*, B, "Self-Consciousness," A; translation modified.

Sense

1. *LA*, Part I, chap. 2, A, 2. *Sinn*, beyond meaning sensible sense or intelligible sense, has a meaning in German that only remains in the French expressions *bon sens* (good sense) and *sens commun* (common sense), and that Hegel here marks: the sense of intellection itself.
2. *PM*, §399, and §400 for the immediately following.
3. Ibid., §490, p. 244.
4. Not to forget also that property is for Hegel only the very first moment of the becoming-self of the ethical subject. Cf. *PM*, §487ff.
5. Ibid., §385.
6. *PN*, §308, p. 158.
7. *PM*, §383, *Zusatz*.
8. *LA*, Introduction. It is thus that Hegel posits the necessity proper to art as the "sensible manifestation" of the idea, which is also to say as the revelation of the sensible in its true form.
9. Ibid., §400, p. 73.
10. Cf., for example, ibid., §§380, 408.
11. Cf. the whole analysis of the syllogism in *SL*, II, §1, chap. 3.

12. *SL*, I, §1, chap. 1, C, 3, Remark, p. 106; translation modified.

13. In accordance with the equivalence long since proposed by Jacques Derrida. This is not the place to enter into the debates and to discuss the multiple choices of various translators. One must mediate these and try to penetrate the thing.

[Unfortunately, there is no such decisive English translation of *Aufhebung*. For the purposes of the present text, we have sometimes just resorted to the term *sublation*—which continues to have the virtue of being a more or less transparent placeholder for the German word; and sometimes we have taken Paul de Man's passing suggestion that *Aufhebung* should be rendered as "up-heaval"—which both renders the German word quite literally (perhaps too literally) and seems to resonate (more even than *la relève*) with Nancy's "restlessness." Cf. Paul de Man, "Hegel on the Sublime," in *Aesthetic Ideology*, ed. and intro. Andrzej Warminski (Minneapolis: University of Minnesota Press, 1996), p. 111.—*Trans.*]

14. ["On peut jouer à dire que le sens de la relève est, ou prend, la relève du sens." The expression "prend la relève" means "to relieve," as in the "relief" that occurs in the—in principle, peaceful—changing of the guard (as, for example, in act 1, scene 1 of *Hamlet*: "For this relief much thanks: 'tis bitter cold, / And I am sick at heart"). "Upheaval," at best, only vaguely touches upon what is suggested by this usage of *relève*—unless one wants to imagine the catastrophe of an "upheaval of the guard" (and what thanks for that?)—*Trans.*]

15. *PS*, C, AA, "Reason," B, a, p. 218.

16. *PM*, §554.

17. Ibid., §555, p. 293.

18. *SL*, III, 3, §3, p. 824.

19. Ibid., p. 843; translation modified.

Desire

1. *SL*, III, §2, Introduction, p. 705.

2. *PP* ["The Philosophical Encyclopedia (For the Higher Class)"], §57, p. 135.

3. Cf., for example, *PM*, §381, *Zusatz* (on the relation between the sexes).

4. Ibid., §385, *Zusatz*.

5. Ibid., §386.

6. *PS*, CC, C.

7. *PM*, §573, pp. 309–10.

8. Undoubtedly, one could make analogous claims about the citation of Schiller that closes *PS*, suspending or abruptly diverting its discourse.

9. *PS*, B, "Self-Consciousness," p. 105.

10. Ibid., C, AA, "Reason," B, a.

11. *PM*, §535: in this text, love is said to be "the essential principle of the State." This does not define an amorous politics, and it supposes that Hegel thinks "the State" as the *sublation* (or up-heaval) of the apparatus of separated power that we designate with this name. In other words, he exposes what will become in our time the primary political theme: no longer the institution and nature of government, but the contradiction of the separation and nonseparation of the "common" considered for itself—and also, consequently, the contradiction of separation and nonseparation *within* being-with-the-other itself. Consequently, through his incontestably naive and dated confidence in a certain model of the state, Hegel also provides the lineaments for a thought of the contradiction of all philosophical *foundation* of the political. But we cannot dwell on this point here.

12. *PS*, B, "Self-Consciousness," A, p. 112.

13. "Speculation" thus reconnects with its usual meaning: "imputation or extrapolation which goes beyond the verifiable givens"; cf. *LL*, §82, *Zusatz*, p. 120; translation modified.

14. *PP* ["Logic (For the Middle Class)"], §5, p. 75.

15. *PS*, B, "Self-Consciousness," A, p. 118.

16. Ibid.

17. Ibid., C, AA, "Reason," C, a, pp. 251–52; translation modified.

18. Ibid., C, AA, "Reason," C, c.

Freedom

1. *PN*, §359, p. 385.

2. *SL*, III, chap. 1, B, p. 612; translation modified.

3. Ibid., Preface to the Second Edition, p. 40.

4. G. W. F. Hegel, *Encyclopedia of the Philosophical Sciences*, Preface to the Second Edition (1827), *LL*, pp. 8–10.

5. *PM*, §423, p. 164; translation modified.

6. *SL*, II, §2, chap. 2, II, A, pp. 503–4. [The citation given is a piecing together of two different passages.—*Trans.*]

7. The sense that Hegel gives to "position" by the "concept": the latter grasps and posits. But what it posits is its own activity.

8. *PS*, BB, "Spirit," C, pp. 364ff.

9. *SL*, III, §3, chap. 3, "The Absolute Idea," p. 843.

10. *PS*, BB, "Spirit," C, pp. 383ff.

11. *PN*, §375. War, which Hegel certainly does not perceive in the same fashion we do, would have to be given particular treatment on its own. [The expression "donner la mort" means to murder or kill; "se donner la mort" would therefore mean to murder oneself. Hence the reference to suicide in the next sentence.— *Trans.*]

12. Cf. *PS*, BB, "Spirit," A, a, pp. 267–78.

13. *SL*, III, §1, chap. 1, A, p. 603. [The citation given here is a compression of two paragraphs, in other words, an "allusion."— *Trans.*]

14. *PM*, §427, then §§428–30, pp. 168–71.

We

1. *PS*, Introduction.

2. Ibid.

3. Ibid. Cf. the opening pages of the Preface.

4. Ibid., Introduction, p. 47; translation modified.

5. Ibid., Preface, p. 12; translation modified.

6. Ibid., p. 20.

7. Ibid., pp. 36, 38.

Selected Texts by G. W. F. Hegel

[Given the absence of any textual indications explaining the precise function of these selected passages in the economy of Nancy's text, one is led to speculate on the author's role in their selection and framing. What is most notable is the fact that these passages are, for the most part, not directly addressed in Nancy's text: it is therefore possible that their selection is not Nancy's at all, but that of an editor. In any case, it is necessary to note that the titles for the passages are certainly not Hegel's: perhaps Nancy's, perhaps another's.— *Trans.*]

Index

Jean-Luc Nancy is professor of philosophy at the University of Strasbourg and the author of several books, including *The Inoperative Community* and *The Sense of the World,* both published by the University of Minnesota Press.

Jason Smith is a doctoral candidate in the Department of Comparative Literature at the University of California–Irvine.

Steven Miller is a doctoral candidate in the Department of Comparative Literature at the University of California–Irvine.